cooking easier, healthier & better

150+ DELICIOUS RECIPES

RULE THE KITCHEN®

3-in-1

COOKING SYSTEM

Nutritional Analyses: Calculations for the nutritional analyses in this book are based on the largest number of servings listed within the recipes. Calculations are rounded up to the nearest gram or milligram, as appropriate. If two options for an ingredient are listed, the first one is used. Not included are optional ingredients or serving suggestions.

Editors: Mona Wetter Dolgov and Ronda DiGugielmo • Graphic Designer: Leslie Anne Feagley
Photo Creative Director: Anne Sommers Welch • Photography: Quentin Bacon • Additional Photography: Gary Sloan and Heath Robbins • Food Stylist: Mariana Velasquez • Recipe Development: Euro-Pro Test Kitchen Team and Culinary Palette, Amy Golino, Kimberly Letizia and Venessa Spillios

Published in the United States of America by
Great Chefs International
New Hope, PA 18938
www.greatchefsinternational.com

ISBN: 978-1-934193-85-3
Printed in China

TABLE OF CONTENTS

YOUR NINJA COOKING SYSTEM
COOKING EASIER, EATING BETTER

One thing almost everybody has in common today: there are tons of things to manage and the clock is always ticking. Wherever we go, whatever we do, it seems like we never have enough time to do the things we want to do. Whether you are a seasoned home chef or a novice in the kitchen trying to get a quick meal on the table, your Ninja 3-in-1 Cooking System will help you make your meals more flavorful and healthier, with ease, speed, and true convenience.

The Ninja 3-in-1 Cooking System with Triple Fusion Heat Technology does it all. This revolutionary advanced system combines oven, stovetop cooking, slow cooking, steam roasting, and baking technology to enhance flavors, making meats juicier, meals healthier, and desserts more moist, and elevating your family meals from ordinary to extraordinary. It puts success on your table with these versatile features:

FAST ONE-POT MEAL MAKING — Now, with your Ninja Cooking System's Triple Fusion Heat, you can make complete meals for your family in just one single pot. You can layer meals and cook pasta, veggies and meats all at the same time — pasta does not even have to be drained! Casseroles come out extra crispy on both the bottom and sides. You can even prepare delicious meals from frozen and take them right to your table in 30 minutes or less. Use either the STOVETOP or Triple Fusion Heat OVEN setting!

STEAM OVEN ROASTING — How to bring out the best quality in practically any cut of meat? Sear first by using STOVETOP HIGH, place meat on roasting rack, and then simply add water to the pot to create a steam infusion. Set to your desired temperature, and begin steam roasting! Steam-infused roasting cuts the cooking time by up to 30% and makes your meats juicier. By adding fresh or dried herbs, broth, or wine to your water, you'll add extra delicious flavors. Try some of our recommended flavor infusions in our chart provided for added inspiration.

STEAM OVEN BAKING — Baking this modern way might be new to you. But it's one more feature that makes the Ninja 3-in-1 Cooking System a true breakthrough appliance. Leave your kitchen oven off. You'll find that steam baking delivers lighter, richer puddings and moist, higher-rising cakes. Plus, you only have to use half the fat! This means healthier, lower-calorie desserts — even at less than 50 calories — using this new revolutionary style to bake!

SEARIOUS/SLOW COOKING — To make more flavorful meals, professional chefs sear meats and sauté vegetables before slow cooking. Until now, that meant an extra step of heating up a second skillet pan, and at least one more pan to wash. The Ninja 3-in-1 Cooking System lets you sear, brown and slow cook meats right in the same appliance, with its built-in stovetop. Plus, the slow cooker is programmable, allowing you to set the cooking time, and it will automatically keep warm once cooking is complete. It's a convenient way to cook, making meal preparation and cleanup easier.

USING THE NINJA COOKING SYSTEM COOKBOOK

This cookbook provides recipes and tips you'll find invaluable. They'll help you use the Ninja 3-in-1 Cooking System to simplify your preparation for all of your meals.

Take a minute to look them over. We've included 150 recipes, each customized for the Ninja 3-in-1 Cooking System, that have all been developed and tested in our Ninja kitchens. The recipes tell you exactly what you need for the dish and how to prepare it — clear directions for reliable success. At the top of each recipe, we explain benefits and best uses. You'll also find at least one tip for healthy ingredient choices, time-saving methods, or serving suggestions.

Eight chapters share the secrets of using the Ninja 3-in-1 Cooking System for exciting results:

30-MINUTE MEALS: Easy meals perfect for a weeknight — fast, satisfying, complete.

LITE FARE (HEALTHY & DELICIOUS): Healthier meals, with an eye on lower calories and fat.

APPETIZERS: Formal starters or yummy party snacks for entertaining.

SOUPS/STEWS: Hearty and savory, even perfect for a lighter meal!

ENTREES: Main courses your family — and even guests — will love.

SIDE DISHES: Speedy, delicious accompaniments all made in one pot!

DESSERTS: Tempting treats made healthier without the need of your home stove.

BREAKFASTS: Surprise! Make the first meal of the day easy and delicious!

Time to get started! Pick a recipe from any chapter and give it a try. We built the Ninja 3-in-1 Cooking System to make your life easier. It's one kitchen appliance that eliminates problems and guesswork. Use it every day to save time while preparing meals you're proud to serve.

Have fun!
The NINJA Kitchen Team

 **Stovetop**

SEAR & SAUTÉ — It's a trick that savvy cooks have known for years — searing and browning meat, and sautéing vegetables develops added flavors, color, and texture to your meals. The result: tender, juicier, more flavorful meats, and sweeter aromatic vegetables. Searing meats especially adds attractive color, crusty texture, and flavor contrast you expect from the best restaurant meals. You can now bring that same quality to your home-cooked meals simply and easily, all in one pot.

For the first time, the Ninja 3-in-1 Cooking System lets you sear, brown, or sauté using the STOVETOP setting. It's quick and simple. Just put the ingredients in the pot, set the Stovetop to the correct setting, and go!

This STOVETOP feature is versatile, too. The LOW setting simmers soups and sauces, MED perfectly sautés aromatics like onions and garlic, browns meats and tender vegetables, and HIGH sears meats just right. Also use the MED and HIGH to prepare a complete skillet or stir-fry dinner, and to reheat dinners, too!

Use the Stovetop setting for sequential cooking — that means, sear meats on STOVETOP HIGH before you slow cook or steam roast to prepare the most delicious meals. This setting will allow your ingredients to lock in the flavor!

Tips & Tricks

1. The preset temperatures are similar to your Stovetop on LOW, MED, or HIGH.

2. Do not use the lid when using the STOVETOP HIGH SETTING TO PREVENT BURNING OF FOOD.

3. Use the STOVETOP MED-HIGH setting to make gravies from your liquids after you roast — all in the same pot!

4. For healthier cooking, remove any excess fat from the cooking pot before roasting. Be sure to wear protective mitts when handling unit.

5. For quicker browning, set to STOVETOP HIGH for 2-3 minutes before placing ingredients in pot.

Fast One-Pot Meal Making

ONE-POT MEALS — Your Ninja 3-in-1 Cooking System's Triple Fusion Heat Technology provides heat to both the sides and bottom of the pot that allows you to create complete meals all at the same time — from Shrimp Scampi to Spaghetti and Meatballs! This means no extra pans for browning foods or preparing more complex dishes. Now, when your meals are complete, you will have only one pot to clean. You can even prepare meals with pasta in the same pot — by layering the foods in the right way, pasta will be ready, without the need to drain!

LAYERED MEALS — For the first time, you can prepare complete meals in a single pot. Even challenging dishes like layered casseroles cook up beautifully with every ingredient done properly — vegetables, crispy toppings, and meats prepared to family-pleasing perfection. The roasting rack included can accommodate the different meal components. Typically, place your starch on the bottom with the appropriate broth or water, and place your protein and vegetables on the roasting rack during cooking. The rack makes it easy to check for doneness, and to remove each meal component when it is perfectly cooked.

Achieve impressive food quality with one-pot convenience!

Tips & Tricks

1. Dense root vegetables cook slower than many meat cuts or more tender veggies. Cut them into small uniform pieces so they'll cook at the same rate as other ingredients.

2. Vegetables can be added with starches in layered meals to add more flavorful dishes.

3. Frozen fish and chicken breasts cook perfectly on the roasting rack or right in the pot, and you can prepare meals in less than 30 minutes.

4. See our charts in the back of the book for cooking guides for meats, vegetables, and starches for inspiration and to manage getting your meals complete at the same time.

EASY SPAGHETTI & MEATBALLS

Searious Slow Cooking

SLOW COOKING — The Ninja 3-in-1 Cooking System is also a SEARious slow cooker — the STOVETOP setting allows you to sear your meats first, then SLOW COOK all in the same appliance! Searing not only gives great texture, it also builds flavor profiles that will elevate your dishes to gourmet quality. The slow cook feature allows you to cook food all day, and it is safe to leave home while cooking! Cook on LOW for all-day cooking, or cook on HIGH in half the time, great for weekend comfort-food cooking. Whether cooking savory Hearty Beef Stew, Pulled Pork & Apple Cider Sliders, or a White Turkey Chili, this portable counter top appliance offers versatile convenience when cooking new and old favorite recipes to treat your family and friends all year long. In addition, use your SEARious slow cooker to make healthier and lighter vegetable dishes too! See all of our delicious recipes!

Tips & Tricks

1. Never fill your pot more than 2/3 full to ensure food is cooked appropriately.

2. Lifting the lid during cooking may increase the total cook time.

3. Because our slow cooking uses very little energy, it is great to slow cook in the hot summer months to keep your kitchen cool.

4. While some frozen foods can be cooked successfully in the slow-cooker mode, it may increase the total cook time. Always use an instant-read thermometer to ensure that foods are cooked to the correct internal temperature. Large frozen roasts are not recommended to be slow cooked. To ensure proper cook time and doneness, it is best to thaw meat safely in the refrigerator before cooking.

5. Certain dried spices can even intensify during slow cooking such as chili pepper powders, cayenne, and red pepper flakes. Use half of the amount of hot spice at the beginning, and add more at the end if necessary.

6. Pouring off or skimming fat that has rendered off during searing or slow cooking will reduce the overall fat content of your dishes to make them healthier for your family.

7. Use the programmability — set the cooking time, and the unit will automatically shift to KEEP WARM until you are ready to enjoy!

PORK CHOPS PROVENÇAL

Steam Oven

STEAM ROASTING — The Ninja 3-in-1 Cooking System has steam-oven capability to make your meats juicier and cut cooking time by up to 30%! The combination of radiant and steam heat makes preparation of poultry, beef, pork, and even fish simple, easy, and delicious. Taking less time and cooking in a steam environment results in juicy, flavorful roasts. You will taste the difference right away…. tender, flavorful perfection.

It's easy to steam roast! Simply add water or flavorful infusion into the pot. Place the roasting rack with your seasoned meat into the pot, set the oven to your desired temperature setting, set the cook time, and start roasting. You will not only save cooking time, but there is also NO PREHEATING REQUIRED!

We've described a series of flavor infusions that actually bring rich taste into the food while it cooks. Check out our flavor-infusion charts in the back of the book for delicious ideas!

Tips & Tricks

1. Spray the roasting rack with nonstick cooking spray before you cook. Meats won't stick and cleanup will be even easier.

2. Arranging foods in even layers on the rack promotes even cooking.

3. Wait 5–10 minutes after roasting meat before you serve, to let the meat rest and the juices settle. The juices distribute evenly, and everything tastes even better.

4. Keep the rack level when you lift it out so food won't slide or roll off.

5. Protect yourself — always use oven mitts or pot holders when you remove the roasting rack.

6. Try roasting with or without the rack. Many cooks make a "rack" of root or aromatic vegetables (like shallots, onion chunks, or potatoes) to support the meat. This adds flavor in both directions.

SWEET & SPICY PORK BABY BACK RIBS

🔲 Steam Baking

STEAM BAKING — The Ninja 3-in-1 Cooking System also steam bakes to make your desserts moister and healthier. By baking in a steam environment, you only have to use HALF the fat, plus you get cakes that are spongier and more delicious. This results in healthier desserts that taste delicious! Prepare tasty cupcakes and loaf cakes — cheesecakes and pudding cakes also taste lighter and more delicious! It's an easy way to indulge, and save calories!

It is really simple to steam bake in the Ninja 3-in-1 Cooking System. Place water at the bottom of the pot. Place your baking pan with batter on the roasting rack, set to OVEN, set your desired temperature and time, and start baking!

Tips & Tricks

1. The pot's nonstick coating makes a great baking surface. You'll only need a nonstick spray if the recipe calls for it.

2. Always use oven mitts or pot holders when you remove the roasting rack from the pot.

3. A handy rule of thumb for steam baking: Add a cup of water for about every 10 minutes of baking time.

4. Fruited topping cakes are made best when the fruit is placed on the bottom of the pan. Lift the cake out of the pan to create delicious fruited upside-down cakes.

MINI CHEESECAKES

COD WITH TOMATO CAPER SAUCE & SUGAR SNAP PEAS

CHAPTER 1:
30-Minute Meals

 STOVETOP

HEARTY SKILLET LASAGNA

Signature

Easiest lasagna ever! Brown meat and cook noodles, then finish it off with spinach and cheeses — all in the same pot! Covered cooking makes this recipe almost foolproof, so you can experiment and try different sauces, greens, and cheeses.

PREP: 5 minutes • **COOK:** 25 minutes • **SERVINGS:** 6

Ingredients

1 pound ground beef

10 uncooked lasagna noodles, broken into 2-inch pieces

1 jar (24 ounces) pasta sauce

1½ cups water

1 package (about 6 ounces) fresh baby spinach

1 cup shredded mozzarella cheese

½ cup ricotta cheese

¼ cup shredded Parmesan cheese

Directions

1. Place beef into pot. Set to STOVETOP HIGH. Cook uncovered 10 minutes or until beef is browned, stirring often.

2. Arrange noodle pieces over beef. Pour sauce and water over noodles. Set to STOVETOP MED. Cover and cook 15–20 minutes or until noodles are tender. Turn off pot.

3. Stir in spinach. Stir cheeses in bowl. Spoon cheese mixture over noodle mixture. Cover and let stand.

NINJA HEALTHY TIP

Replace ground beef with ground turkey or chicken and add 1 tablespoon olive oil to pot before browning. Also, substitute part-skim mozzarella cheese and low-fat or even fat-free ricotta for those listed in the recipe.

 OVEN

Signature

EASY SPAGHETTI & MEATBALLS

The perfect combination of ingredients means that pasta, meatballs, and sauce can cook together in the pot — no prep needed! This family favorite is a true one-dish meal.

PREP: 5 minutes • **COOK:** 25 minutes • **SERVINGS:** 4

Ingredients

4 cups water

1 pound spaghetti, broken in half

1 jar (24 ounces) pasta sauce (for thinner sauce, reduce water by ¼ cup)

1 package (24 ounces) frozen meatballs

Directions

1. Pour 4 cups water into pot. Stir in spaghetti, sauce, and meatballs. Set OVEN to 300°F for 25 minutes. Cover and cook until pasta is tender and meatballs are hot, stirring occasionally. NOTE: When using thinner sauces, use 3¾ cup water. For whole grain and thicker pastas, increase cooking time by 2–5 minutes, or until pasta is tender. Serve immediately.

NINJA SERVING TIP

Serve with a tossed green salad and garlic bread.

STOVETOP/STEAM OVEN

Signature

CHICKEN PICCATA

Sautéed chicken breasts, quinoa cooked with lemon and wine and perfectly steamed asparagus, cooked in 30 minutes using only one pot! Layered cooking makes it easy to serve a homemade meal in minutes.

PREP: 5 minutes • **COOK:** 25 minutes • **SERVINGS:** 4

Ingredients

2 tablespoons all-purpose flour

¼ teaspoon salt

⅛ teaspoon ground black pepper

1¼ pounds boneless, skinless, thin-sliced chicken breast halves

2 tablespoons olive oil

2 tablespoons butter

1 cup chicken broth

1 cup dry white wine

⅓ cup lemon juice

¼ cup brined capers, rinsed and drained

1 cup uncooked quinoa, rinsed

1¼ pounds fresh asparagus, cut into ½-inch pieces

Directions

1. Stir flour, salt, and black pepper on plate. Coat chicken with flour mixture.

2. Add oil and butter to pot. Set to STOVETOP HIGH and heat until butter is melted. Add chicken to pot. Cook uncovered 10 minutes or until chicken is lightly browned on both sides. Remove chicken from pot and place on roasting rack.

3. Add broth, wine, lemon juice, and capers to pot. Stir in quinoa. Place rack with chicken in pot, and place asparagus on rack with chicken. Set OVEN to 300°F for 15 minutes. Cover until chicken is cooked through, asparagus is tender, and quinoa breaks apart.

4. Remove asparagus and chicken from pot. Stir quinoa mixture. Turn off pot. Let quinoa mixture stand. Garnish with parsley.

NINJA HEALTHY TIP

Artichokes are a great source of fiber. Stir 1 package (about 9 ounces) frozen artichoke hearts in with the capers in step 3.

STOVETOP/STEAM OVEN

Signature

QUICK SHRIMP SCAMPI

This amazing dish needs almost no prep time! Add uncooked pasta to garlic-wine sauce and stir in frozen shrimp to finish heating at the same time the pasta is cooking.

PREP: 5 minutes • **COOK:** 25 minutes • **SERVINGS:** 4

Ingredients

4 tablespoons butter

4 cloves garlic, minced

¼ teaspoon crushed red pepper

1 cup chopped fresh parsley

Salt and ground black pepper

½ cup dry white wine

4 cups water

1 package (1 pound) angel hair pasta, broken in half

1 pound frozen cooked, peeled, and deveined large shrimp

Directions

1. Place butter into pot. Set to STOVETOP HIGH and heat until butter is melted. Stir in garlic, red pepper, **half** the parsley, salt, and black pepper into pot. Cook uncovered 5 minutes or until garlic is lightly browned, stirring occasionally.

2. Add wine, water and pasta to pot. Stir to submerge pasta in liquid. Set OVEN to 300°F for 15 minutes. Cover and cook.

3. Add shrimp into pot. Set time for another 10 minutes. Cover and cook until pasta is tender and shrimp are heated through. Sprinkle with remaining parsley.

NINJA TIME-SAVER TIP

Try garlic that is already chopped, sold in jars in the produce department.

◎ STOVETOP

CASHEW CHICKEN WITH BLACK BEAN SAUCE & SNOW PEAS

This sophisticated dish cooks quickly in one pot. The richer flavor of chicken thighs is delicious browned, then simmered with vegetables and black bean sauce. Cashews add both flavor and texture.

PREP: 5 minutes • **COOK:** 25 minutes • **SERVINGS:** 4

Ingredients

1 tablespoon olive oil

6 skinless, boneless chicken thighs

1 onion, chopped

1 red pepper, chopped

3 cloves garlic, chopped

1 cup diced tomatoes

2 tablespoons black bean sauce

½ cup cashew nuts

1 cup fresh snow peas

Directions

1. Pour oil into pot. Set STOVETOP HIGH and heat oil. Add chicken to pot. Cook uncovered 10 minutes or until browned on both sides. Remove chicken from pot.

2. Add onion, pepper, and garlic to pot. Cook 2 minutes. Stir in tomatoes and black bean sauce. Return chicken to pot. Sprinkle with nuts. Cover and cook 10-20 minutes or until chicken is cooked through. Stir in snow peas during last 5 minutes of cooking time.

NINJA SERVING TIP

Serve over hot cooked white or brown rice.

 STOVETOP

GREEK STYLE CHICKEN & VEGETABLE PITAS

The filling for these fresh-tasting sandwiches is amazingly quick to make. Chicken is browned for color and flavor, then layered with vegetables to finish cooking simultaneously.

PREP: 5 minutes • **COOK:** 25 minutes • **SERVINGS:** 4

Ingredients

⅓ cup lemon juice

2 tablespoons vegetable or olive oil

1 teaspoon dried oregano leaves, crushed

½ teaspoon ground cumin

1½ pounds skinless, boneless chicken breast halves, cut into cubes

½ pint grape tomatoes

1 yellow squash or green zucchini, cut in half lengthwise, then into 1-inch slices

4 pita breads

Directions

1. Stir lemon juice, oil, oregano, and cumin in bowl. Place chicken and **½ cup** lemon mixture in another bowl and toss to coat. Add tomatoes and squash to remaining lemon mixture and toss to coat.

2. Place chicken into pot. Set to STOVETOP HIGH. Cook uncovered 5–10 minutes or until chicken is browned, stirring constantly. Stir zucchini mixture into pot. Cover and cook 10–15 minutes or until zucchini is tender and chicken is cooked through.

3. Divide chicken and zucchini mixture among pita breads.

NINJA TIME-SAVER TIP

Buy cut-up zucchini at the salad bar in your grocery store!

27

STOVETOP

CHEESE PIEROGIES WITH KIELBASA

Onion, garlic, and chicken broth make a savory sauce to coat hearty pierogies and kielbasa. No need to thaw pierogies first — the nonstick surface of the pot keeps pierogies from sticking and makes for easier cleanup!

PREP: 5 minutes • **COOK:** 25 minutes • **SERVINGS:** 4

Ingredients

¼ cup olive oil

1 large onion, chopped

2 cloves garlic, minced

1 package fully-cooked, turkey kielbasa (about 13 ounces), cut into ½-inch slices

1 package (16 ounces) frozen potato and Cheddar cheese pierogies

1 cup chicken broth

1 tablespoon chopped fresh parsley (optional)

Directions

1. Pour **2 tablespoons** oil into pot. Set to STOVETOP HIGH and heat oil. Add onion and garlic to pot. Cook uncovered 5 minutes or until onion is tender, stirring often. Stir in kielbasa. Cook uncovered 5 minutes, stirring often.

2. Add remaining oil and pierogies to pot and stir to coat. Cook uncovered 10 minutes or until pierogies and kielbasa are browned, stirring often with a wooden spoon. Pour broth into pot. Cover and cook 5 minutes. Sprinkle with parsley, if desired.

NINJA SERVING TIP

Try other flavors of pierogies for a change of pace.

STOVETOP

STIR-FRIED BEEF & BROCCOLI WITH CELLOPHANE NOODLES

This flavorful stir-fry is quick to make, served over easy-to-make noodles. Cellophane noodles are sometimes called "bean threads" and can be found in the international foods section of most markets.

PREP: 10 minutes • **COOK:** 15 minutes • **SERVINGS:** 4

Ingredients

1 tablespoon vegetable oil

1 pound boneless sirloin beef steak, cut into thin strips

1 clove garlic, minced

1 tablespoon grated fresh ginger

4 cups fresh broccoli florets

¾ cup water

⅛ cup oyster or hoisin sauce

2 tablespoons soy sauce

1 tablespoon rice wine vinegar

1 tablespoon cornstarch

1 package (4 ounces) cellophane noodles, reconstituted according to package directions

Directions

1. Pour oil into pot. Set to STOVETOP HIGH and heat oil. Add beef, garlic, and ginger and cook uncovered 10 minutes or until beef is browned, stirring often. Add broccoli and cook 1 minute.

2. Stir water, oyster sauce, soy sauce, vinegar, and cornstarch in bowl. Add to beef mixture and stir to coat. Cover and cook 3 minutes or until broccoli is tender. Serve beef mixture over noodles.

NINJA SERVING TIP

Serve over rice instead of cellophane noodles for a more traditional twist. For a change of pace, replace broccoli with bell peppers and asparagus or replace beef with chicken strips.

OVEN

COD WITH TOMATO CAPER SAUCE & SUGAR SNAP PEAS

The delicate flavor of cod pairs perfectly with the more assertive flavors of capers, garlic, and basil in the sauce. This flavorful liquid keeps the cod moist and helps cook the sugar snap peas to the perfect tender-crisp texture.

PREP: 5 minutes • **COOK:** 20 minutes • **SERVINGS:** 4

Ingredients

2 medium tomatoes, chopped

½ cup white wine

2 tablespoons drained capers

2 cloves garlic, minced

1 tablespoon chopped fresh basil leaves

½ teaspoon salt

4 cod fillets (about 1 pound)

¾ pound sugar snap peas

Directions

1. Stir tomatoes, wine, capers, garlic, basil, and salt in pot. Add fish to pot. Set OVEN to 375°F for 10 minutes; cover.

2. Place snap peas on fish. Set OVEN to 375°F for 10 minutes. Cover and cook until fish flakes easily when tested with a fork and snap peas are tender-crisp.

NINJA TIME-SAVER TIP

Substitute 1 can (14.5 ounces) diced tomatoes in juice for chopped tomatoes.

STOVETOP

CREAMY CHICKEN & MUSHROOMS

This classic chicken dish features a homemade mushroom cream sauce cooked in the same pot as the chicken. This is not only convenient, but it intensifies the flavor, thanks to the browned bits in the bottom of the pot.

PREP: 5 minutes • **COOK:** 25 minutes • **SERVINGS:** 4

Ingredients

1¼ pounds boneless, skinless chicken breasts

Salt and ground black pepper

2 tablespoons butter

1 small onion, chopped

1 package (8 ounces) sliced mushrooms

1 clove garlic, minced

½ teaspoon salt

½ teaspoon thyme

2 tablespoons flour

1 cup chicken broth

½ cup white wine

2 tablespoons heavy cream

Directions

1. Season chicken with salt and black pepper.

2. Place chicken into pot. Set to STOVETOP HIGH and heat pan. Cook uncovered 10 minutes or until chicken is browned on both sides. Remove chicken from pot.

3. Add butter and onion to pot. Set to STOVETOP MED. Cook uncovered 3 minutes or until onion is tender, stirring occasionally.

4. Add mushrooms, garlic, salt, and thyme to pot. Cook 4 minutes or until vegetables are tender, stirring occasionally. Stir in flour. Cook 1 minute, stirring constantly. Stir in broth and wine and heat to a boil.

5. Return chicken to pot. Cook uncovered 5 minutes or until chicken is cooked through. Stir in cream.

 HEALTHY TIP

Substitute 2% milk or evaporated skim milk for the heavy cream. Serve with a fresh green salad with low-fat dressing.

32

 STEAM OVEN

SALMON WITH ARUGULA & SUN-DRIED TOMATO COUSCOUS

Substitute any leafy green, such baby spinach, if arugula is unavailable. Dark green leafy vegetables, such as arugula, **are great sources for vitamins A, C, and K, folate, iron, calcium and fiber.**

PREP: 10 minutes • **COOK:** 20 minutes • **SERVINGS:** 4

Ingredients

1½ tablespoons olive oil

1 small onion, chopped

1 cup uncooked couscous

1 cup water

¼ cup sun-dried tomatoes, cut in ¼-inch strips

1 pint grape tomatoes, cut in half

Cooking spray

4 salmon fillets (6 ounces each)

1 package (7 ounces) fresh arugula

Directions

1. Set OVEN to 350°F. Heat oil and stir in onion. Cook uncovered 5 minutes or until onion is tender, stirring occasionally. Stir in couscous, water, sun-dried tomatoes, and grape tomatoes.

2. Spray roasting rack with cooking spray and place into pot. Place fish on rack. Cover and cook 10–20 minutes (depending on fish thickness) or until fish flakes easily when tested with fork. Remove fish from pot, cover, and keep warm. Turn off pot.

3. Stir arugula into pot. Serve couscous mixture with fish.

 **NINJA** TIME-SAVER TIP

Look for onions already chopped in the produce section.

STOVETOP

CAVATELLI & BROCCOLI ALFREDO

This classic Italian dish is made with cavatelli right from the freezer. There's no need to thaw or cook separately — it all cooks right in one pot.

PREP: 5 minutes • **COOK:** 25 minutes • **SERVINGS:** 4

Ingredients

1 tablespoon olive oil

1 small onion, chopped

2 cloves garlic, minced

1 package (about 14 ounces) frozen cavatelli

4 cups broccoli florets

1 jar (15 ounces) light Alfredo sauce

2 cups water

¼ cup shredded Parmesan cheese

Directions

1. Pour oil into pot. Set to STOVETOP HIGH and heat oil. Stir in onion and garlic. Cook uncovered 5 minutes or until onion is tender, stirring occasionally.

2. Stir in cavatelli, broccoli, sauce, and water. Set to STOVETOP MED. Cover and cook 20 minutes or until cavatelli and broccoli are tender. Stir in cheese just before serving.

NINJA SERVING TIP

Frozen tortellini can replace cavatelli, and asparagus and roasted red peppers can replace broccoli for an alternative dish. Adding ¼ cup diced prosciutto also makes a tasty variation.

STOVETOP/OVEN

STUFFED ZUCCHINI

Tender zucchini halves stuffed with a pancetta and Parmesan-seasoned filling can be a light entrée or a substantial side dish for your next dinner party.

PREP: 10 minutes • **COOK:** 20 minutes • **SERVINGS:** 6

Ingredients

3 medium zucchini, cut in half lengthwise

3 teaspoons olive oil

½ cup diced pancetta

1 red pepper, chopped

2 cloves garlic, minced

1 teaspoon dried oregano leaves, crushed

2 tablespoons chopped fresh parsley

Salt and freshly ground black pepper

½ cup Japanese-style bread crumbs (panko)

½ cup grated Parmesan cheese

Directions

1. Scoop pulp from zucchini halves, leaving ¼-inch shells. Chop zucchini pulp.

2. Pour **1 teaspoon** oil into pot. Set to STOVETOP HIGH and heat oil. Add pancetta. Cook uncovered for about 5 minutes or until almost crisp, stirring often. Stir in chopped zucchini pulp, red pepper, garlic, and oregano. Cook uncovered for about 5 minutes, stirring occasionally.

3. Remove vegetable mixture to bowl. Stir in parsley, salt and black pepper, bread crumbs, and **half** the cheese. Spoon vegetable mixture into zucchini halves. Sprinkle with remaining cheese.

4. Pour remaining oil into pot. Place stuffed zucchini into pot in single layer. Set OVEN to 400°F for 20 minutes, checking after 15 minutes. Cover and cook until zucchini is tender.

NINJA HEALTHY TIP

Omit pancetta and only use half the Parmesan cheese. Serve as a plated first course.

 STOVETOP

CHEDDAR-STUFFED BURGERS WITH BARBEQUE DIJON ONIONS

Simple and inexpensive ingredients combine to create bistro-worthy burgers in 30 minutes. Your family and friends will vote this recipe as one of their favorites.

PREP: 15 minutes • **COOK:** 15 minutes • **SERVINGS:** 4

Ingredients

1 pound ground beef

4 cubes (1-inch) Cheddar cheese

Salt and ground black pepper

2 teaspoons canola oil

2 medium onions, chopped

¼ cup barbeque sauce

1 tablespoon Dijon mustard

4 potato sandwich rolls

Directions

1. Shape beef into 4 burgers. Make an indentation in center of each burger and place **1 piece** cheese in **each**. Press beef to enclose cheese. Season burgers with salt and black pepper.

2. Pour **1 teaspoon** oil into pot. Set to STOVETOP HIGH and heat oil. Stir in onions. Cook uncovered 5 minutes or until onions are tender, stirring occasionally. Stir in barbeque sauce and mustard. Cook uncovered 1 minute or until hot. Move onion mixture to one side of pot.

3. Add remaining oil and burgers to pot. Cook uncovered 9 minutes or until burgers are cooked through, turning over once halfway through cooking time. Serve burgers and onion mixture on rolls.

NINJA TIME-SAVER TIP

Look in your grocer's freezer case for frozen onions already chopped or in the produce section or salad bar.

STOVETOP/STEAM OVEN

HERB-ROASTED PORK TENDERLOINS & POTATOES

Cook a delicious complete meal, all in one pot! Since you'll want to make this often, you can vary the flavor by substituting your favorite seasonings for the lemon pepper.

PREP: 5 minutes • **COOK:** 25 minutes • **SERVINGS:** 6

Ingredients

1 pound red potatoes, cut in quarters

1 large onion, cut into wedges

1 pound baby carrots

2 tablespoons olive oil

1 tablespoon lemon pepper seasoning

2 pork tenderloins (about 2½ pounds)

1 cup chicken broth

2 tablespoons chopped fresh parsley

Directions

1. Place potatoes, onion, and carrots in bowl. Add **1 tablespoon** oil and **1 teaspoon** lemon pepper seasoning and toss to coat.

2. Rub pork with remaining oil and season with remaining lemon pepper seasoning. Place pork into pot. Set to STOVETOP HIGH. Cook uncovered 10 minutes or until pork is browned on all sides. Remove pork from pot.

3. Pour broth into pot. Add potato mixture. Place roasting rack into pot and place pork on rack. Set OVEN to 375°F for 20 minutes, checking after 15 minutes. Cover and cook until pork is cooked through. Remove pork from pot. Let meat rest before slicing.

NINJA TIME-SAVER TIP

Look for baby or small red potatoes and avoid the step of cutting them into quarters.

STOVETOP

PIZZA PASTA WITH PEPPERONI

The whole family will love this dish — it's a meat-lovers' pizza in a bowl! The pasta cooks right in the sauce, so you can make a salad while it's cooking, then get everything to the table together.

PREP: 5 minutes • **COOK:** 25 minutes • **SERVINGS:** 4

Ingredients

1 pound ground beef

1 small onion, chopped

½ of a 1-pound package uncooked rotini pasta

1 jar (24 ounces) pasta sauce

2 cups water

⅛ of a 6-ounce package sliced pepperoni

2 cups shredded mozzarella cheese

Directions

1. Set pot to STOVETOP HIGH. Add beef and onion to pot. Cook uncovered 10 minutes or until beef is browned, stirring often.

2. Stir in pasta, sauce, and water. Set to STOVETOP MED. Cook uncovered 15–20 minutes or until pasta is tender, stirring occasionally.

3. Stir in pepperoni and **1 cup** cheese. Sprinkle with remaining cheese. Turn off pot. Cover and let stand 3 minutes.

NINJA HEALTHY TIP

For a lighter dish, try substituting ground turkey for the ground beef. Just add 1 tablespoon olive oil before browning.

 **STOVETOP**

TOFU, SHIITAKE, & RED PEPPER STIR-FRY

Dusting the tofu with cornstarch gives it a great texture when fried, crispy on the outside and softer in the center.

PREP: 10 minutes • **COOK:** 15 minutes • **SERVINGS:** 4

Ingredients

- 1 package extra-firm tofu, cut into 1"-2" pieces and drained on paper towels

- 5 tablespoons cornstarch, (3 tablespoons for tofu, 2 tablespoons for sauce)

- 3-5 tablespoons canola or vegetable oil, separated

- 2 red peppers, sliced thin

- 1 cup shiitake mushrooms, sliced thin

- 1 bunch of whole scallions, sliced thin on the diagonal, reserving

- 3 cloves of garlic, chopped

- 1 tablespoon fresh ginger, chopped

- ¾ cup vegetable broth

- 3 tablespoons soy sauce

- 1 tablespoon rice wine vinegar

- 2 teaspoons sugar

- Salt and black pepper

Directions

1. In a small bowl, dust the tofu in the cornstarch, covering all sides.

2. On STOVETOP HIGH, heat the oil. Add the tofu and brown on all sides, adding more oil if necessary. Once all of the tofu has been browned (approximately 5 minutes), remove and set aside.

3. Cook the red peppers, shiitake mushrooms, and scallions, stirring frequently until they have softened, about 5 minutes. Set aside. Add a tablespoon of oil and cook the garlic and ginger until fragrant but not browned.

4. Add the ingredients for the sauce and bring to a boil, stirring frequently until the sauce thickens to desired consistency, 5–10 minutes. Add the cooked tofu and vegetables to the sauce, stirring to combine. Season to taste with salt and pepper and serve.

NINJA SERVING TIP

This dish can be served with cellophane rice noodles that simply need to be soaked in hot water.

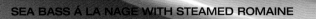

SEA BASS Á LA NAGE WITH STEAMED ROMAINE

CHAPTER 2:
Lite Fare

 **STEAM OVEN**

Signature

APRICOT & COUNTRY MUSTARD SALMON

The liquid in the bottom of the pot keeps the salmon moist and flavorful. This dish has amazing flavor and it's surprisingly easy to make — with ingredients right from your pantry.

PREP: 5 minutes • **COOK:** 10 minutes • **SERVINGS:** 4

Ingredients

2 cups water

¼ cup apricot preserves

2 tablespoons country Dijon-style mustard

1½ pounds salmon fillets

Salt and ground black pepper

Directions

1. Stir preserves and mustard in bowl.

2. Pour 2 cups of water into pot. Season fish with salt and black pepper. Place fish on roasting rack. Spread preserve mixture on fish. Place rack into pot.

3. Set OVEN to 400°F for 20 minutes (for thick fillets), checking after 10–15 minutes for desired doneness.

   NUTRITION PER SERVING: 290 CALORIES; 12G FAT; 2.5G SATURATED FAT; 180MG SODIUM; 13G CARBOHYDRATE; 0G FIBER; 32G PROTEIN

NINJA SERVING TIP

Sprinkle the fish with sliced green onion and serve with baked potatoes and a green salad.

 **STOVETOP**

HOT & SOUR SHRIMP SAUTÉ

Forget take-out — this restaurant-worthy recipe is ready in 25 minutes! When buying fresh ginger, use a 1-inch peeled piece to make the minced tablespoon needed here. Wrap what's left and store it in the freezer for several months.

PREP: 15 minutes • **COOK:** 10 minutes • **SERVINGS:** 4

Ingredients

1 tablespoon packed brown sugar

1 tablespoon cornstarch

¾ cup water or vegetable broth

3 tablespoons rice wine vinegar

2 tablespoons soy sauce

1 tablespoon vegetable oil

¾ pound uncooked medium shrimp, peeled and deveined

1 tablespoon minced fresh ginger

2 cloves garlic, minced

¼ teaspoon crushed red pepper

1 package (about 3.5 ounces) sliced shiitake mushrooms

1 large red bell pepper, cut into thin strips

3 green onions, finely chopped

Directions

1. Stir brown sugar and cornstarch in bowl. Add water, vinegar, and soy sauce and stir until smooth.

2. Pour oil into pot. Set to STOVETOP HIGH and heat oil. Add shrimp, ginger, garlic, and crushed red pepper. Cook uncovered 2 minutes. Add mushrooms and bell pepper. Cook 2 minutes, stirring occasionally.

3. Stir in vinegar mixture. Cover and cook 2 minutes or until shrimp are cooked through, stirring occasionally. Stir in green onions. Serve shrimp mixture over rice.

NUTRITION PER SERVING: 220 CALORIES; 4G FAT; 0.5G SATURATED FAT; 1130MG SODIUM; 29G CARBOHYDRATE; 1G FIBER; 16G PROTEIN.

NINJA SERVING TIP

Serve the shrimp mixture over hot cooked white rice or rice noodles.

STOVETOP

ASIAN LETTUCE WRAPS

Savor warm, well-flavored chicken wrapped with cool and
refreshing lettuce and you will race back for more.
So easy and quick to make!

PREP: 10 minutes • **COOK:** 15 minutes • **SERVINGS:** 4

Ingredients

1 pound lean ground chicken or
turkey

1 small onion, chopped

2 cloves garlic, minced

1 tablespoon minced fresh ginger

¼ cup hoisin sauce

1 tablespoon soy sauce

1 tablespoon sriracha
(spicy chili sauce) (optional)

1 can (8 ounces) water chestnuts,
drained and finely chopped

¼ cup chopped fresh cilantro leaves

16 Bibb or Boston lettuce leaves

Directions

1. Place chicken into pot. Set to STOVETOP HIGH. Cook
uncovered 5 minutes or until chicken is cooked through,
stirring often.

2. Stir in onion, garlic, and ginger. Cook 5 minutes or until onion
is tender, stirring occasionally. Stir in hoisin sauce, soy sauce,
sriracha sauce, if desired, and water chestnuts. Cover and cook
2 minutes or until mixture is hot, stirring occasionally. Stir
in cilantro.

3. Divide chicken among lettuce leaves. Fold lettuce around filling.

**NUTRITION PER SERVING: 240 CALORIES; 10G FAT; 2.5G SATURATED FAT;
590MG SODIUM; 16G CARBOHYDRATE; 2G FIBER; 21G PROTEIN**

NINJA SERVING TIP

Instead of wrapping chicken mixture
in lettuce leaves, serve as a salad
with chicken mixture spooned over
shredded lettuce or bok choy.

CHICKEN & QUINOA SALAD

Quinoa is an ancient grain high in protein with a nutty flavor.
This recipe has three sources of protein but only one pot for
cooking!

PREP: 10 minutes • **COOK:** 20 minutes • **SERVINGS:** 4

Ingredients

1 pound skinless, boneless chicken
  tenderloins

Salt and ground black pepper

2 cups water

1 cup uncooked quinoa, rinsed

¾ cup frozen shelled soybeans,
  thawed

¾ cup cherry tomatoes, cut in half

⅓ cup chopped walnuts

½ cup chopped parsley

3 tablespoons extra-virgin olive oil

2 tablespoons rice wine vinegar

Directions

1. Season chicken with salt and black pepper.

2. Stir water and quinoa in pot. Set to STOVETOP HIGH. Cover and cook until water heats to a boil.

3. Place chicken on roasting rack and place rack into pot. Set OVEN to 325°F for 15 minutes, checking after 10 minutes. Cover and cook until chicken is cooked through. Remove rack and chicken from pot. Cover chicken to keep warm.

4. Cover pot and cook 5 minutes or until quinoa is tender yet chewy and all water is absorbed. Turn off pot. Stir in soybeans, tomatoes, walnuts, parsley, olive oil, and vinegar. Season with salt and black pepper. Serve with chicken.

NUTRITION PER SERVING: 520 CALORIES; 25G FAT; 3.5G
SATURATED FAT; 70MG SODIUM; 34G CARBOHYDRATE;
6G FIBER; 39G PROTEIN

 HEALTHY TIP

Substitute your favorite low-calorie
vinaigrette dressing for the oil and vinegar
in this recipe. Lima beans and peas can
also be substituted for soybeans.

STOVETOP

CHICKEN, FETA, & SUN-DRIED TOMATO BURGERS

Heat in the pot surrounds chicken patties, seasoned with feta and sun-dried tomatoes for a well-seared outside and moist flavor sealed inside.

PREP: 10 minutes • **COOK:** 10 minutes • **STAND:** 5 minutes • **SERVINGS:** 4

Ingredients

1 pound ground chicken

⅓ cup crumbled feta cheese

⅓ cup drained chopped sun-dried tomatoes in olive oil; reserve 1 tablespoon oil

5 sprigs fresh oregano, chopped

Salt and ground black pepper

4 multigrain hamburger buns

8 tablespoons low-fat (2%) plain Greek yogurt

1 cup baby arugula leaves

Directions

1. Stir chicken, cheese, tomatoes, and oregano in bowl. Season with salt and black pepper. Shape chicken mixture into 4 burgers.

2. Pour reserved tomato oil into pot. Place burgers into pot. Set to STOVETOP HIGH. Cook uncovered 2 minutes or until burgers are browned on both sides. Cover and cook 5 minutes or until burgers are cooked through. Remove burgers from pot and let stand 5 minutes.

3. Spread yogurt on tops of buns. Place burgers on buns. Top with arugula.

NUTRITION PER SERVING: 390 CALORIES; 20G FAT; 6G SATURATED FAT; 440MG SODIUM; 23G CARBOHYDRATE; 2G FIBER; 29G PROTEIN

NINJA SERVING TIP

You can also use ground turkey instead of chicken and watercress in place of arugula.

 STOVETOP/SLOW COOK

CITRUS MARINATED PORK CHOPS

Browning pork in the pot after marinating and before slow cooking adds a rich caramelized flavor to this finished dish.

PREP: 10 minutes • **MARINATE:** 2 hours • **COOK:** 4 hours, 5 minutes • **SERVINGS:** 6

Ingredients

2 cups chicken broth

⅔ cup olive oil

⅔ cup orange juice

8 cloves garlic, chopped

8 strips each orange zest and lemon zest

2 sprigs fresh rosemary

2 teaspoons salt

1 teaspoon ground black pepper

6 boneless pork chops, ¾-inch thick

Directions

1. Stir broth, oil, juice, garlic, zest, rosemary, salt, and black pepper in bowl. Reserve **half** the broth mixture. Pour remaining broth mixture into resealable gallon-size plastic bag. Add pork and turn to coat. Seal bag and refrigerate 2 hours.

2. Remove pork from marinade. Discard marinade. Set pot to STOVETOP HIGH. Add pork to pot in batches. Cook uncovered 5 minutes or until pork is lightly browned on both sides.

3. Pour reserved broth mixture over pork. Set to SLOW COOK HIGH for 4 to 5 hours. Cover and cook until pork is tender.

NUTRITION PER SERVING: 260 CALORIES; 18G FAT; 4G SATURATED FAT; 570MG SODIUM; 3G CARBOHYDRATE; 0G FIBER; 22G PROTEIN

NINJA SERVING TIP

Serve over rice tossed with chopped parsley and lemon zest.

STOVETOP

MINTED PEA SOUP

This beautiful green soup is perfect for that special spring luncheon and is fresh-tasting and ready in only 30 minutes.

PREP: 5 minutes • **COOK:** 25 minutes • **SERVINGS:** 4

Ingredients

2 tablespoons butter

1 large onion, chopped

3 cups chicken broth

3 cups frozen peas

⅓ teaspoon ground black pepper

¼ cup packed fresh mint leaves

Directions

1. Place butter into pot. Set to STOVETOP HIGH and heat until butter is melted. Stir in onion. Cook uncovered 10 minutes or until onion is tender, stirring occasionally. Stir in broth, peas, and black pepper and heat to a boil.

2. Set pot to STOVETOP MED. Cover and cook 5 minutes or until peas are tender. Stir mint into pot.

3. Make sure soup is cooled, and pour soup in batches to blender, making sure the jar is 2/3 full at a time. Puree soup mixture using a blender until smooth. Place soup back in pot. Set to STOVETOP MED. Cook uncovered 5 minutes or until soup is hot.

NUTRITION PER SERVING: 170 CALORIES; 7G FAT; 3.5G SATURATED FAT; 810MG SODIUM; 19G CARBOHYDRATE; 6G FIBER; 7G PROTEIN

NINJA SERVING TIP

Great served with a dollop of sour cream.

STOVETOP/STEAM OVEN

Lite Fare

SALMON WITH HERBED CAPER SAUCE & GREEN BEANS

Sautéed shallots cook in the bottom of the pot with wine and capers while the salmon and green beans steam on the rack above. The aromatic steam infuses the fish with flavor and steams the beans to perfect crispness.

PREP: 10 minutes • **COOK:** 40 minutes • **SERVINGS:** 6

Ingredients

1 tablespoon olive oil

1 shallot, finely chopped

2 cups reduced-sodium chicken broth

¼ cup dry white wine

½ of a 3.5-ounce bottle capers, rinsed and drained

⅛ teaspoon ground black pepper

3 (5-ounce) frozen salmon fillets, cut into 6 serving-sized pieces

½ teaspoon lemon pepper seasoning

1 package (12 ounces) fresh whole green beans

2 tablespoons cold water

1 tablespoon cornstarch

2 tablespoons thinly sliced fresh basil leaves

Directions

1. Pour oil into pot. Set to STOVETOP HIGH and heat oil. Add shallot to pot. Cook uncovered 5 minutes until shallot is tender, stirring occasionally. Stir in broth, wine, capers, and black pepper.

2. Place roasting rack into pot. Place fish on rack. Sprinkle with lemon pepper seasoning. Place green beans on fish. Set to OVEN 350°F for 20 minutes. Cover and cook until fish flakes easily when tested with fork and green beans are tender-crisp. Remove fish and green beans from pot, cover, and keep warm.

3. Stir water and cornstarch in bowl until smooth. Stir cornstarch mixture into pot set to STOVETOP MED and cook uncovered 8 minutes or until mixture boils and thickens, stirring often. Stir in basil. Serve fish with sauce and beans.

NUTRITION PER SERVING: 220 CALORIES; 10G FAT; 2G SATURATED FAT; 270MG SODIUM; 8G CARBOHYDRATE; 2G FIBER; 24G PROTEIN

NINJA SERVING TIP

Complete this delicious, healthy meal with hot cooked rice or quinoa.

SEA BASS Á LA NAGE WITH STEAMED ROMAINE

This dish is healthful yet packed with flavor. The fish and romaine are layered in the pot and cook at the same time, while the sauce cooks in the bottom. It's perfect for a summer dinner party.

PREP: 20 minutes • **COOK:** 15 minutes • **SERVINGS:** 4

Ingredients

1 lemon

4 sea bass fillets, skin removed (about 1 pound)

Salt and ground black pepper

3 tablespoons butter

1 tablespoon minced shallot

2 garlic cloves, minced

½ cup white wine

½ cup chicken stock

2 hearts of romaine, cut in half lengthwise

2 teaspoons sliced fresh chives

Directions

1. Grate zest and squeeze juice from lemon. Season fish with salt and ground black pepper.

2. Place butter into pot. Set to STOVETOP HIGH and heat until butter is melted. Add shallot and garlic to pot. Cook uncovered 1 minute. Stir in wine and cook 2 minutes or until slightly reduced. Stir in stock and lemon zest and season with salt and black pepper.

3. Place fish on roasting rack and place rack into pot. Place romaine on top of fish. Season with salt and black pepper. Set OVEN to 425°F for 10 minutes. Cover and cook until fish flakes easily when tested with fork and romaine is tender-crisp.

4. Remove rack with fish and romaine from pot. Stir lemon juice into pot. Serve romaine topped with fish and drizzled with stock mixture. Sprinkle with chives.

NUTRITION PER SERVING: 230 CALORIES; 11G FAT; 6G SATURATED FAT; 210MG SODIUM; 4G CARBOHYDRATE; 1G FIBER; 22G PROTEIN

NINJA SERVING TIP

Use whichever white wine you prefer in this recipe, and serve the rest with dinner! Chardonnay will lend a more buttery flavor, while Riesling will add a sweeter, more fruity note.

 **STOVETOP**

SAUTÉED CHICKEN BREASTS WITH CITRUS SALSA

Quick-cooking chicken seasoned in lime juice, then served with sweet and spicy salsa, will have your family calling for this great dish over and over.

PREP: 20 minutes • **COOK:** 20 minutes • **SERVINGS:** 4

Ingredients

1 large orange, cut in half and sectioned, reserving juice

1 medium grapefruit, cut in half and sectioned, reserving juice

⅓ cup chopped red onion

3 tablespoons lime juice

1 tablespoon chopped fresh cilantro leaves

½ jalapeño pepper, seeded and minced

1 tablespoon honey

1 tablespoon ground cumin

1 teaspoon ground coriander

½ teaspoon kosher salt

2 cloves garlic, minced

1 tablespoon canola oil

4 boneless, skinless chicken breast halves

Directions

1. Coarsely chop orange and grapefruit sections. Stir orange, grapefruit, reserved juices, onion, **1 tablespoon** lime juice, cilantro, jalapeño pepper, and honey in bowl.

2. Stir remaining lime juice, cumin, coriander, salt, and garlic in another bowl. Rub chicken with garlic mixture.

3. Pour oil into pot. Set to STOVETOP HIGH and heat oil. Add chicken and cook 12 minutes or until chicken is browned on both sides and cooked through, turning over once halfway through cooking time. Serve with citrus salsa.

NUTRITION PER SERVING: 250 CALORIES; 7G FAT; 1G SATURATED FAT; 310MG SODIUM; 18G CARBOHYDRATE; 2G FIBER; 28G PROTEIN

NINJA SERVING TIP

Serve with fresh spinach salad with low-fat dressing.

 **STOVETOP**

SEARED SIRLOIN WITH ROMESCO SAUCE

Sirloin steaks are seared right in pot, then topped with a powerhouse steak sauce — a twist on pesto — for a simple yet spectacular main dish.

PREP: 10 minutes • **COOK:** 12 minutes • **SERVINGS:** 4

Ingredients

¼ cup smoked almonds

½ cup diced tomatoes

½ cup jarred roasted red peppers

1 tablespoon red wine vinegar

1 tablespoon smoked paprika

1 teaspoon anchovy paste

1 clove garlic

4 tablespoons olive oil

Salt

2 pounds boneless beef sirloin,
  cut into 4 pieces

Directions

1. Place almonds into food processor. Cover and process until finely ground. Add tomatoes, peppers, vinegar, paprika, anchovy paste, and garlic. Cover and process until smooth. With processor running, add **2 tablespoons** oil slowly until sauce is thickened. Stir in salt.

2. Add remaining oil to pot. Set to STOVETOP HIGH and heat oil. Add beef. Cook uncovered 15 minutes for medium or until desired doneness, turning beef over once halfway through cooking time. Serve beef with sauce.

NUTRITION PER SERVING: 450 CALORIES; 28G FAT; 6G SATURATED FAT; 310MG SODIUM; 6G CARBOHYDRATE; 2G FIBER; 44G PROTEIN

NINJA SERVING TIP

Serve with hot cooked rice or baked potato and a simple mixed-greens salad.

Lite Fare

EASY SHEPHERD'S PIE

Comfort food is so convenient when you make it in one pot and have fewer pans to clean up. Use leftovers to create variations on this tasty theme.

PREP: 10 minutes • **COOK:** 30 minutes • **SERVINGS:** 6

Ingredients

- 1½ pounds ground turkey or lean ground beef
- 2 teaspoons steak seasoning
- 1 bag (12 ounces) frozen mixed vegetables (corn, peas, carrots, green beans)
- 2 tablespoons all-purpose flour
- 6 cups prepared mashed potatoes
- 1 cup shredded Cheddar cheese

Directions

1. Add turkey to pot and sprinkle with seasoning. Set to STOVETOP HIGH. Cook uncovered 5 minutes or until turkey is browned, stirring often. Stir in vegetables and flour. Cook uncovered 5 minutes, stirring occasionally.

2. Spread potatoes over turkey mixture. Top with cheese. Set OVEN to 350°F for 20 minutes. Cover and cook until mixture is hot.

NUTRITION PER SERVING: 550 CALORIES; 26 FAT; 9G SATURATED FAT; 1180MG SODIUM; 46G CARBOHYDRATE; 5G FIBER; 33G PROTEIN

NINJA SERVING TIP

Why not keep the comfort idea going and serve prepared tapioca pudding from the deli for dessert?

STOVETOP/STEAM OVEN

SPAGHETTI SQUASH WITH TURKEY SAUSAGE

The flesh of cooked spaghetti squash separates into shreds resembling thin spaghetti, making it a great alternative to cooked pasta. Sausage cooks in the pot, then the squash is baked until tender and the "spaghetti" can be scraped out.

PREP: 10 minutes • **COOK:** 50 minutes • **SERVINGS:** 6

Ingredients

1 pound Italian-style turkey sausage, casing removed

2 cups water

1 large spaghetti squash (about 4 pounds), cut in half lengthwise and seeds removed

2 tablespoons grated Parmesan cheese

2 teaspoons no-salt garlic and herb seasoning

1 large tomato, chopped

1 cup packed baby spinach leaves

¼ cup shredded mozzarella cheese

Directions

1. Set pot to STOVETOP HIGH. Add sausage to pot. Cook uncovered 10 minutes or until browned, stirring often. Remove sausage from pot. Spoon off fat.

2. Pour water into pot. Place roasting rack into pot. Place squash, cut side down, on rack. Set OVEN to 425°F for 25 minutes. Cover and cook until squash is tender. Remove squash and rack from pot and let cool 5 minutes.

3. Using fork, scrape flesh from squash and add to pot. Sprinkle with **1 tablespoon** Parmesan cheese and **1 teaspoon** garlic and herb seasoning. Top with sausage, tomato, spinach, and remaining Parmesan cheese and seasoning. Set OVEN to 425°F for 15 minutes. Cover and cook until mixture is hot and bubbling. Sprinkle with mozzarella cheese.

NUTRITION PER SERVING: 150 CALORIES; 6G FAT; 2G SATURATED FAT; 350MG SODIUM; 10G CARBOHYDRATE; 2G FIBER; 13G PROTEIN

 SERVING TIP

Delicious topped with fresh ground or cracked black pepper.

STOVETOP

CANTONESE STEAMED CHICKEN

Steaming the chicken results in a wonderfully tender texture
that's infused with the flavors of soy sauce, honey, and ginger.
The vegetables and sauce cook in the bottom of the pot and
create that delicious scented steam.

PREP: 5 minutes • **COOK:** 25 minutes • **SERVINGS:** 4

Ingredients

2 tablespoons soy sauce

1 tablespoon rice wine vinegar

1 tablespoon minced fresh ginger

1 tablespoon honey

¼ teaspoon crushed red pepper

4 thin-sliced chicken breasts
 (about 1 pound)

1 tablespoon vegetable oil

1 medium onion, sliced

2 carrots, sliced ¼ inch thick

8 ounces sugar snap peas, strings
 removed

6 shiitake mushrooms, stemmed and
 sliced

½ cup chicken broth

Directions

1. Stir soy sauce, vinegar, ginger, honey, and crushed red pepper in bowl. Add chicken and toss to coat.

2. Pour oil into pot. Set to STOVETOP HIGH and heat oil. Add onions, carrots and cook uncovered 7 minutes, stirring occasionally.

3. Remove chicken from soy sauce mixture and place on roasting rack. Stir soy sauce mixture and chicken broth in pot with onions and carrots. Place roasting rack into pot. Cover and cook 5 minutes. Add sugar snap peas and mushrooms, and cook another 7–10 minutes until chicken is cooked through and vegetables are just tender.

NUTRITION PER SERVING: 190 CALORIES; 6G FAT; 1G SATURATED FAT; 680MG SODIUM; 10G CARBOHYDRATE; 1G FIBER; 25G PROTEIN

NINJA SERVING TIP

Serve the chicken and vegetable mixture over hot cooked rice or noodles and sprinkle with sliced fresh chives.

 **STOVETOP**

LIGHT & LUSCIOUS LINGUINE CARBONARA

Lite Fare

This twist on traditional carbonara has all the flavor but none of the guilt! The creamy, cheesy sauce comes together quickly in one pot, ready to toss with the hot linguine!

PREP: 10 minutes • **COOK:** 25 minutes • **SERVINGS:** 4

Ingredients

1 package (6 ounces) turkey bacon, chopped

1 small onion, chopped

4 cloves garlic, minced

1 cup low-fat milk

½ of an 8-ounce package reduced-fat cream cheese

¼ teaspoon ground black pepper

½ cup reduced-sodium chicken broth

1 tablespoon flour

½ of a 1-pound package linguine, cooked and drained

¼ cup grated Parmesan cheese

½ cup chopped fresh basil leaves

Directions

1. Add bacon to pot. Set to STOVETOP HIGH. Cook uncovered 12 minutes or until bacon is browned, stirring occasionally. Remove bacon from pot and drain on paper towels.

2. Add onion and garlic to pot. Cook uncovered 5 minutes or until onion is tender, stirring often. Stir in milk, cream cheese, and black pepper, stirring often, until cream cheese is melted.

3. Set pot to STOVETOP MED. Stir chicken broth and flour in bowl. Stir broth mixture into pot and heat to a boil, stirring occasionally. Cook uncovered 5 minutes or until mixture is thickened, stirring often.

4. Add pasta to pot and toss to coat. Stir in bacon, Parmesan cheese and basil.

NUTRITION PER SERVING: 450 CALORIES; 17G FAT; 7G SATURATED FAT; 840MG SODIUM; 53G CARBOHYDRATE; 3G FIBER; 22G PROTEIN

NINJA SERVING TIP

Great with addition of 1 cup frozen peas added with the broth mixture.

TILAPIA PUTTANESCA

A few items from your pantry combine to make a flavor-packed sauce to spoon over tilapia. The tomato, olive, and caper sauce cooks in the pot while the infused steam rises to season and cook the fish perfectly.

PREP: 15 minutes • **COOK:** 18 minutes • **SERVINGS:** 4

Ingredients

1 pound tilapia fillets

Salt and ground black pepper

2 tablespoons olive oil

3 garlic cloves, chopped

1 can (28 ounces) Italian plum tomatoes, drained and crushed

Crushed red pepper

10 pitted kalamata olives, chopped

2 tablespoons capers, drained and rinsed

1 teaspoon dried oregano leaves, crushed

Directions

1. Season fish with salt and black pepper.

2. Pour oil into pot. Set to STOVETOP HIGH and heat oil. Add fish to pot. Cook uncovered 5 minutes. Turn fish over and cook 2 minutes more. Remove fish from pot.

3. Add garlic to pot. Cook uncovered 1 minute, stirring often. Stir in tomatoes, red pepper, olives, capers, and oregano. Place roasting rack into pot. Place fish on rack. Set OVEN to 350°F for 5 minutes. Cover and cook until fish flakes easily when tested with fork. Serve fish with sauce.

NUTRITION PER SERVING: 260 CALORIES; 14G FAT; 2G SATURATED FAT; 490MG SODIUM; 9G CARBOHYDRATE; 1G FIBER; 24G PROTEIN

NINJA SERVING TIP

Serve the fish and hearty sauce with a side of hot cooked linguine.

STEAM OVEN/STOVETOP

TOFU & BROCCOLI TERIYAKI

Tofu sautéed in the pot takes on flavors of garlic and teriyaki and the tender broccoli completes this quick and simple-to-make meatless dish.

PREP: 10 minutes • **COOK:** 25 minutes • **SERVINGS:** 4

Ingredients

2 cups water

6 cups fresh broccoli florets

1 package (14 ounces) extra-firm tofu, drained and cut into 1-inch cubes

Salt and ground black pepper

2 tablespoons canola oil

3 cloves garlic, minced

½ teaspoon crushed red pepper

½ cup reduced-sodium teriyaki sauce

Directions

1. Pour water into pot. Place broccoli in roasting rack and place rack into pot. Set to OVEN 350°F. for 15 minutes. Cover and cook until broccoli is bright green and tender. Remove broccoli and rack from pot and drain on paper towels. Discard water from pot. Wipe pot dry, allowing it to cool before handling.

2. Pat tofu dry and season with salt and black pepper. Place oil, tofu, and garlic into pot. Cook uncovered 5 minutes or until tofu is golden brown on bottom. Turn tofu over. Add red pepper and pour teriyaki sauce over tofu. Set to STOVETOP HIGH. Cover and cook 5 minutes or until tofu is browned.

3. Add broccoli to tofu mixture and stir to coat. Season with salt and black pepper.

NUTRITION PER SERVING: 200 CALORIES; 11G FAT; 1.5G SATURATED FAT; 680MG SODIUM; 14G CARBOHYDRATE; 4G FIBER; 12G PROTEIN

NINJA HEALTHY TIP

Serve with hot cooked brown rice and fresh pineapple.

STUFFED FILLET OF SOLE

Delicate sole is stuffed with a fresh chopped cucumber tomato mixture, then steamed with a lemon-wine broth. Steaming locks in the nutrients and flavor, and the savory broth is ladled over the fish before serving.

PREP: 15 minutes • **COOK:** 20 minutes • **SERVINGS:** 4

Ingredients

1 cup chopped seedless cucumber

½ cup grape tomatoes, chopped

1 green onion, thinly sliced

2 tablespoons chopped fresh basil leaves

Salt or ground black pepper

4 sole or flounder fillets (about 1 pound)

1 tablespoon olive oil

1 cup chicken broth

½ cup white wine

2 tablespoons lemon juice

Directions

1. Stir cucumber, tomatoes, green onion, and basil in bowl. Season with salt and black pepper. Divide cucumber mixture among fish fillets. Roll up fish around filling and secure with wooden picks.

2. Pour oil into pot. Set to STOVETOP HIGH and heat oil. Add fish and cook uncovered 3 minutes or until lightly browned on both sides. Remove fish from pot.

3. Stir broth, wine, and lemon juice in pot. Place fish on roasting rack and place roasting rack into pot. Set OVEN to 375°F for 15 minutes. Cover and cook until fish flakes easily when tested with fork. Serve broth mixture over fish.

NUTRITION PER SERVING: 170 CALORIES; 5G FAT; 1G SATURATED FAT; 310MG SODIUM; 4G CARBOHYDRATE; 0G FIBER; 22G PROTEIN

NINJA HEALTHY TIP

Serve fish and sauce with hot cooked couscous and a spinach salad.

STOVETOP

SEARED SCALLOP SALAD WITH GRAPEFRUIT & AVOCADO

Thanks to the even heat in this pot, searing scallops is so easy. You will love the unexpected flavor combination of grapefruit, avocado, and honey.

PREP: 15 minutes • **COOK:** 6 minutes • **SERVINGS:** 4

Ingredients

1 grapefruit, cut in half and sectioned, reserving juice

1 avocado, pitted, peeled, and thinly sliced

1 shallot, minced

3 tablespoons honey

2 tablespoons white wine vinegar

1 tablespoon canola oil

Salt and ground black paper

1 tablespoon butter

12 large sea scallops

1 head Boston or Bibb lettuce

Directions

1. Stir grapefruit sections and avocado in bowl. Stir reserved grapefruit juice, shallot, honey, vinegar, oil, salt, and black pepper in another bowl.

2. Add butter to pot. Set to STOVETOP HIGH and heat butter until melted and very hot. Add scallops to pot. Cook uncovered 6 minutes or until browned on both sides and cooked through, turning over once halfway through cooking time.

3. Arrange lettuce on platter and top with grapefruit and avocado. Top with scallops and drizzle with grapefruit juice mixture.

NUTRITION PER SERVING: 280 CALORIES; 14G FAT; 3.5G SATURATED FAT; 100MG SODIUM; 28G CARBOHYDRATE; 5G FIBER; 10G PROTEIN

NINJA HEALTHY TIP

Use canola oil or reduced-fat butter instead of butter to sear scallops.

STOVETOP/OVEN

TURKEY CUTLETS WITH BRAISED FENNEL & ORANGE

Brown turkey cutlets, then braise fennel in honey-orange sauce — no need for a separate skillet and saucepan — it's all done in one pot!

PREP: 15 minutes • **COOK:** 45 minutes • **SERVINGS:** 6

Ingredients

1¾ pounds boneless turkey breast, sliced horizontally into ¼-inch thick fillets

Salt and ground black pepper

½ cup flour

3 tablespoons olive oil

2 fennel bulbs, cut into ½-inch slices

1½ cups orange juice

2 tablespoons honey

Directions

1. Season turkey with salt and black pepper. Coat turkey with flour.

2. Pour oil into pot. Set to STOVETOP HIGH and heat oil. Add turkey in batches to pot. Cook uncovered 10 minutes or until turkey is browned. Remove turkey from pot.

3. Add **half** the fennel to pot and season with salt and black pepper. Set to STOVETOP HIGH. Cook uncovered 5 minutes or until fennel is golden brown. Remove fennel from pot. Repeat with remaining fennel. Return cooked fennel to pot.

4. Add orange juice and honey to pot. Set OVEN to 250°F for 15 minutes. Cover and cook until fennel is tender, and orange juice mixture is reduced and thickened slightly.

5. Return turkey to pot and turn to coat. Set to STOVETOP HIGH. Cook uncovered 5 minutes or until turkey is cooked through, stirring occasionally.

NUTRITION PER SERVING:
300 CALORIES; 8G FAT;
1G SATURATED FAT; 90MG
SODIUM; 27G CARBOHYDRATE;
3G FIBER; 30G PROTEIN

NINJA SERVING TIP

Add chopped fennel fronds and orange segments as a tasty and colorful garnish.

PULLED PORK & APPLE CIDER SLIDERS

CHAPTER 3:
Appetizers

 STOVETOP

WARM & SPICY WHITE BEAN & ARTICHOKE DIP

This rich, Tuscan-inspired dip is simple to make with ingredients right from your pantry.

PREP: 15 minutes • **COOK:** 25 minutes • **SERVINGS:** 36

Ingredients

2 tablespoons olive oil

2 medium onions, diced

4 cloves garlic, minced

2 packages (8 ounces each) Neufchâtel or light cream cheese, cut up

2 cans (9 ounces each) artichoke hearts, drained and coarsely chopped

2 cans (about 15 ounces each) cannellini beans, rinsed, drained, and coarsely mashed

½ cup milk

2 teaspoons cayenne pepper sauce

½ cup grated Parmesan cheese

Salt and ground black pepper

1 tablespoon chopped fresh parsley (optional)

Directions

1. Pour oil into pot. Set to STOVETOP HIGH and heat oil. Add onions to pot. Cook uncovered 5 minutes or until onions are tender, stirring often. Add garlic to pot. Cook 2 minutes, stirring constantly.

2. Stir cream cheese, artichokes, beans, milk, and pepper sauce into pot. Set to STOVETOP MED. Cover and cook 10 minutes or until cream cheese is melted, stirring occasionally. Stir in Parmesan cheese. Season with salt and black pepper. Sprinkle with parsley, if desired.

 **NINJA** SERVING TIP

Serve warm with assorted fresh vegetables and/or crackers.

OVEN

BUFFALO CHICKEN POPPERS

These yummy snacks have all the flavor of buffalo chicken in one tidy little package that bakes perfectly in the pot! Chicken, hot pepper sauce, celery, and blue cheese wrapped in warm flaky crescent dough — they're irresistible!

PREP: 10 minutes • **COOK:** 10 minutes • **SERVINGS:** 8

Ingredients

¼ cup butter, melted

¼ cup cayenne pepper sauce

1 cup finely chopped rotisserie chicken

1 stalk celery, finely chopped

2 tablespoons crumbled blue cheese

1 package (8 ounces) refrigerated crescent rolls

Directions

1. Stir butter, pepper sauce, chicken, celery, and cheese in bowl.

2. Separate crescent rolls into **8** dough triangles, then cut triangles in half. Press down gently to flatten each triangle half. Place **2 tablespoons** chicken mixture in center of each triangle half. Pull one corner at a time up over the filling to enclose the filling.

3. Place filled dough into pot. Set OVEN to 375°F for 10 minutes. Cover and cook until poppers are golden brown, turning over once halfway through cooking time.

 SERVING TIP

Serve with blue cheese or ranch dressing and cut-up celery for dipping.

STOVETOP/SLOW COOK

CAPONATA & GOAT CHEESE CROSTINI

Eggplant, onion, and garlic slow cook to melt-in-your-mouth tenderness, their rich flavor balanced by tart capers, creamy goat cheese, and crunchy pine nuts.

PREP: 15 minutes • **COOK:** 4 hours, 5 minutes • **SERVINGS:** 32

Ingredients

2 tablespoons olive oil

1 eggplant (about 2 pounds), unpeeled, cut into ½-inch pieces

1 medium onion, chopped

4 cloves garlic, chopped

1 can (29 ounces) diced tomatoes, undrained

2 tablespoons balsamic or red wine vinegar

¼ cup capers or chopped pitted oil-cured olives

2 baguettes, sliced and toasted

4 ounces crumbled goat cheese

Toasted pine nuts

Shredded fresh basil leaves

Directions

1. Place oil, eggplant, onion, and garlic into pot. Set to STOVETOP HIGH. Cook uncovered 5 minutes or until onion is tender, stirring occasionally.

2. Stir in tomatoes, vinegar, and capers. Set to SLOW COOK HIGH for 4 to 5 hours. Cover and cook until eggplant is very tender.

3. Stir eggplant mixture and serve on toasted baguette slices with goat cheese, pine nuts, and basil sprinkled on top.

NINJA SERVING TIP

Serve any leftover caponata over pasta for a quick and easy meatless meal.

 **STOVETOP/STEAM OVEN**

CHICKEN & VEGETABLE SKEWERS WITH THAI COCONUT SAUCE

These wonderful little skewers are perfect for dipping and cook at the same time as the dipping sauce itself! Party-ready in no time.

PREP: 20 minutes • **COOK:** 15 minutes • **SERVINGS:** 8

Ingredients

1 lime

24 wooden picks

1 onion, cut into ½-inch pieces

1 pound skinless, boneless chicken breast halves, cut into 1-inch pieces

1 red pepper, cut into ½-inch pieces

Salt and ground black pepper

2 tablespoons canola oil

2 cloves garlic, minced

1 piece (1-inch) fresh ginger, peeled and minced

1 teaspoon red curry paste

1 can (13.5 ounces) coconut milk

2 tablespoons cornstarch

2 tablespoons cold water

Fresh cilantro leaves

Directions

1. Grate zest and squeeze juice from lime.

2. Thread **1 piece** onion, **1 piece** chicken, and **1 piece** red pepper on **each** wooden pick. Season with salt and black pepper.

3. Stir oil, garlic, ginger, and curry paste into pot. Set to STOVETOP HIGH. Cook uncovered 2 minutes or until garlic and ginger are tender, stirring occasionally. Stir in coconut milk and lime zest. Season with salt and black pepper.

4. Place skewers on roasting rack. Place roasting rack into pot. Set OVEN to 350°F for 10 minutes. Cover and cook until chicken is cooked through. Remove skewers and rack from pot.

5. Stir cornstarch, water, and lime juice in bowl. Stir cornstarch mixture into pot. Set to STOVETOP HIGH. Cook uncovered 2 minutes or until mixture is thickened, stirring constantly. Season with salt and black pepper.

6. Serve skewers with coconut sauce. Garnish with cilantro leaves.

NINJA SERVING TIP

Toss leftover Thai coconut sauce with cilantro and cooked soba noodles or linguine the next day for lunch.

 **STOVETOP**

CHILI CHICKEN MANGO SKEWERS

Chicken cooks in only 6 minutes in garlic, jalapeño, and spicy chili sauce. Sweet chunks of mango and fresh cilantro leaves balance the spice in these tempting little appetizers.

PREP: 30 minutes • **COOK:** 6 minutes • **SERVINGS:** 10

Ingredients

1 pound boneless, skinless chicken breast halves, cut into 1-inch pieces

Salt and freshly ground black pepper

2 tablespoons canola oil

2 cloves garlic, minced

1 jalapeño pepper, seeded and minced

2 tablespoons sriracha (spicy chili sauce)

3 ripe mangoes, peeled, cut into 1-inch pieces

30 wooden picks

30 fresh cilantro leaves

Directions

1. Season chicken with salt and black pepper.

2. Add oil, garlic, and jalapeño pepper to pot. Set to STOVETOP HIGH. Cook uncovered 1 minute or until pepper is tender. Stir in chicken. Cook uncovered 5 minutes or until chicken is cooked through, stirring occasionally. Stir in sriracha. Cook for 1 minute. Remove chicken from pot.

3. Thread **1 piece** mango, **1 leaf** cilantro, and **1 piece** chicken on each wooden pick.

NINJA SERVING TIP

Substitute beef steak, cut into 1-inch strips, for chicken for another great appetizer.

SLOW COOK

PULLED PORK & APPLE CIDER SLIDERS

Slow cooking guarantees tender pork. Braised with cider and spicy mustard, these pulled pork sliders make indulgent little sandwiches that are perfect served with baked sweet potato fries.

PREP: 10 minutes • **COOK:** 5 hours • **SERVINGS:** 6

Ingredients

- 1 boneless pork shoulder roast (3 to 4 pounds)
- Salt and ground black pepper
- 2 teaspoons paprika
- ¼ cup spicy brown mustard
- ¼ cup packed brown sugar
- 3 cloves garlic, minced
- 1 cup apple cider or apple juice
- 1 package (15 ounces) slider or mini sandwich buns (12 mini buns)

Directions

1. Season pork with salt, black pepper, and paprika. Stir mustard, brown sugar, garlic, and cider in pot. Add pork and turn to coat. Set to SLOW COOK HIGH for 5 to 6 hours. Cover and cook until pork is fork-tender.

2. Transfer pork into large bowl. Using two forks, shred pork. Spread additional mustard on buns, if desired. Divide pork mixture among buns.

NINJA TIME-SAVER TIP

Keep this meal quick and simple and serve with sweet potato fries from the freezer section and sliced fresh cucumber with ranch dressing for dipping.

 SLOW COOK

MULLED SPICED CRANBERRY APPLE CIDER

Using whole spices like cinnamon sticks and cloves adds depth of flavor to this simple combination of juices. Slow cooking ensures that flavors balance and meld beautifully.

PREP: 5 minutes • **COOK:** 4 hours • **SERVINGS:** 16

Ingredients

2 quarts cranberry juice

2 quarts apple cider or apple juice

3 cinnamon sticks

1 teaspoon whole cloves

1 teaspoon ground nutmeg

Directions

1. Place all ingredients into pot. Set to SLOW COOK HIGH for 4 to 5 hours. Cover and cook.

NINJA TIME-SAVER TIP

To jump-start recipe heat cider on STOVETOP HIGH.

 OVEN

CHILI CHEESE CORN MUFFINS

These little flavor-packed muffins add punch to any appetizer platter or even the simplest meal. Consistent heat in the pot helps keep muffins moist and tender.

PREP: 10 minutes • **COOK:** 25 minutes • **SERVINGS:** 6

Ingredients

Cooking spray

¾ **cup yellow cornmeal**

¼ **cup all-purpose flour**

1 **tablespoon sugar**

1 **teaspoon baking powder**

½ **teaspoon salt**

1 **egg**

½ **cup sour cream**

¼ **cup butter, melted**

½ **cup shredded Cheddar cheese**

¼ **cup corn**

2 **tablespoons chopped canned green chilies**

2 **tablespoons chopped fresh cilantro leaves**

Directions

1. Spray 6-cup muffin pan with cooking spray. Stir cornmeal, flour, sugar, baking powder, and salt in a bowl. Add egg, sour cream, butter, cheese, corn, chilies, and cilantro and stir until just combined. Spoon batter into muffin-pan cups.

2. Place pan into pot, on rack. Set OVEN to 425°F for 25 minutes. Cover and cook until wooden pick inserted in centers comes out clean. Remove pan from pot. Let muffins cool 5 minutes.

NINJA SERVING TIP

Serve with cilantro butter. Stir ¼ cup softened butter with 1 tablespoon cilantro and ¼ teaspoon grated lime zest.

STOVETOP/STEAM OVEN

CHICKEN SATAY

In only 25 minutes you will have seasoned chicken skewers ready for dipping into a beautiful creamy sauce cooked at the same time!

PREP: 10 minutes • **COOK:** 15 minutes • **SERVINGS:** 8

Ingredients

16 wooden skewers

Cooking spray

1 pound boneless, skinless chicken tenderloins, cut in half lengthwise

¼ teaspoon cayenne pepper

½ teaspoon ground ginger

Salt and ground black pepper

2 tablespoons canola oil

2 cloves garlic, minced

14 ounce can of coconut milk

3 tablespoons creamy peanut butter

1½ tablespoons reduced-sodium soy sauce

3 tablespoons packed light brown sugar

Fresh cilantro leaves

Directions

1. Spray skewers with cooking spray. Thread chicken onto skewers. Season with cayenne pepper, ginger, salt, and black pepper.

2. Add oil and garlic to pot. Set to STOVETOP HIGH. Cook uncovered 1 minute or until garlic is tender, stirring often. Stir coconut milk, peanut butter, soy sauce, and brown sugar into pot. Season with salt and black pepper.

3. Place skewers on roasting rack. Place rack into pot. Set OVEN to 325°F for 10 minutes, checking after 5 minutes. Cover and cook until chicken is cooked through. Remove skewers from pot, cover, and keep warm.

4. Cook coconut milk mixture uncovered 5 minutes or until thickened, stirring often. Serve skewers with sauce for dipping. Sprinkle with cilantro.

NINJA HEALTHY TIP

Substitute reduced-fat broccoli cheese soup, skim milk, and 2% milk cheddar cheese for a lighter version.

Appetizers

BROCCOLI CHEESE DIP

This is no ordinary broccoli dip! Sautéed onion provides a savory base, then broccoli, cheese and seasonings slow cook until the mixture is hot and the flavors are blended. A bit of sun-dried tomato pesto adds the perfect tasty twist.

PREP: 10 minutes • **COOK:** 2 hours, 10 minutes • **SERVINGS:** 6

Ingredients

- 1 tablespoon olive oil

- 1 medium onion, chopped

- 4 cups chopped fresh broccoli

- 1 can (10¾ ounces) condensed broccoli cheese soup

- ½ cup milk

- 1 tablespoon Worcestershire sauce

- 1 tablespoon sun-dried tomato pesto sauce

- 1 cup shredded Cheddar cheese

- Ground black pepper

Directions

1. Pour oil into pot. Set to STOVETOP HIGH and heat oil. Add onion to pot. Cook uncovered 5 minutes or until onion is tender-crisp, stirring occasionally. Add broccoli to pot. Cook 5 minutes, stirring occasionally.

2. Stir soup, milk, Worcestershire, pesto sauce, cheese and black pepper into pot. Set to SLOW COOK LOW for 2 hours. Cover and cook until broccoli is tender and cheese is melted.

NINJA HEALTHY TIP

Substitute reduced-fat broccoli cheese soup and 2% milk Cheddar cheese for the versions in the recipe.

 STOVETOP

SPICED NUTS

Mixed nuts are glazed with a spicy brown sugar coating and sprinkled with fresh orange zest. The pot's nonstick surface makes cleanup fuss-free.

ppetizers

PREP: 2 minutes • **COOK:** 5 minutes • **SERVINGS:** 10

Ingredients

1 orange

1 can (10 ounces) mixed nuts

2 tablespoons canola oil

2 tablespoons packed light brown sugar

½ teaspoon cayenne pepper

¼ teaspoon ground cumin

1 teaspoon ground cinnamon

1 tablespoon water

Directions

1. Grate zest from orange. Line rimmed baking sheet with parchment paper.

2. Place nuts, oil, brown sugar, cumin, cayenne pepper, cinnamon and water into pot. Set to STOVETOP MED. Cook uncovered 5 minutes or until sugar is melted and sugar mixture coats nuts, stirring constantly.

3. Spread nut mixture on baking sheet. Sprinkle with orange zest. Let stand 10 minutes or until sugar mixture is hardened.

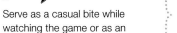 SERVING TIP

Serve as a casual bite while watching the game or as an upscale snack for a cocktail party.

 STOVETOP/OVEN

STUFFED ARTICHOKE BOTTOMS

You can prepare the sautéed mushroom filling, then bake the stuffed artichokes all in one pot! So convenient and easy to clean up.

PREP: 10 minutes • **COOK:** 25 minutes • **SERVINGS:** 6

Ingredients

2 tablespoons olive oil

8 ounces cremini mushrooms, minced

½ cup Japanese-style bread crumbs (panko)

½ cup grated Parmesan cheese

¼ cup chopped fresh parsley

2 cans (14 ounces each) artichoke bottoms, drained

Directions

1. Add oil and mushrooms to pot. Set to STOVETOP HIGH. Cook uncovered 5 minutes or until mushrooms are tender, stirring occasionally. Stir in bread crumbs, cheese, and parsley. Spoon **about 1 tablespoon** mushroom mixture into **each** artichoke bottom.

2. Place filled artichokes into pot. Set OVEN to 350°F for 20 minutes. Cover and cook until artichokes are heated through.

NINJA HEALTHY TIP

These stuffed mushroom and cheese-filled artichokes are a perfect plated first course for your dinner party.

STOVETOP/OVEN

SAUSAGE STUFFED BABY PORTOBELLO MUSHROOMS

This classic dish for entertaining has never been easier to make. Cook sausage filling, then bake the stuffed mushrooms in the same pot!

PREP: 20 minutes • **COOK:** 35 minutes • **SERVINGS:** 7

Ingredients

- 1 package (16 ounces) baby portobello mushrooms
- 1 package (12 ounces) mild Italian sausage, casing removed
- 1 small green or red pepper, chopped
- 1 small onion, chopped
- 1 stalk celery, chopped
- 2 cloves garlic, minced
- ¼ cup Italian-seasoned dry bread crumbs
- ¼ cup grated Parmesan cheese
- ⅛ teaspoon ground black pepper

Directions

1. Separate mushroom stems from mushroom caps. Reserve mushroom caps. Finely chop mushroom stems to make ½ cup.

2. Place sausage, green pepper, onion, celery, chopped mushroom stems, and garlic into pot. Set to STOVETOP HIGH. Cook uncovered 12 minutes or until sausage is cooked through and vegetables are tender, stirring occasionally.

3. Turn off pot. Stir in bread crumbs, **2 tablespoons** cheese, and black pepper. Spoon filling mixture into reserved mushroom caps. Place stuffed mushrooms on roasting rack.

4. Wipe inside or pot with paper towel, allowing it to cool before handling. Place rack into pot. Set OVEN to 425ºF for 25 minutes. Cover and cook until mushrooms are tender. Sprinkle with remaining Parmesan cheese.

NINJA SERVING TIP

For a zestier filling, use hot Italian sausage instead of mild.

STOVETOP/SLOW COOK

KOREAN CHICKEN WINGS

The blend of soy sauce, brown sugar, garlic, and ginger doesn't only coat these wings; slow cooking intensifies the flavor and helps permeate the meat, making them delicious through and through.

PREP: 10 minutes • **COOK:** 3 hours, 5 minutes • **SERVINGS:** 4

Ingredients

2 pounds chicken wings, tips removed

½ cup soy sauce

¼ cup packed brown sugar

3 cloves garlic, minced

2 tablespoons peeled, chopped fresh ginger

3 green onions, thinly sliced

Directions

1. Set pot to STOVETOP HIGH. Add chicken to pot. Cook uncovered 5 minutes or until chicken is lightly browned on both sides.

2. Stir soy sauce, brown sugar, garlic, ginger, and green onions in bowl. Pour soy sauce mixture over chicken and toss to coat. Set to SLOW COOK LOW for 3 to 5 hours. Cover and cook until chicken is cooked through.

NINJA SERVING TIP

Double the recipe for a great party dish and keep warm in pot on SLOW COOK BUFFET.

 STOVETOP

CURRIED SHRIMP SKEWERS WITH CILANTRO

Tender shrimp cooked in peanut oil, curry, garlic, and ginger, and served with fresh green cilantro leaves creates an exotic appetizer.

PREP: 12 minutes • **COOK:** 5 minutes • **SERVINGS:** 8

Ingredients

1 pound uncooked large shrimp, peeled, deveined, tails removed

Salt and ground black pepper

3 tablespoons peanut oil

2 teaspoons curry powder

2 cloves garlic, minced

1 tablespoon minced fresh ginger

Wooden picks

Fresh cilantro leaves

Directions

1. Season shrimp with salt and black pepper.

2. Place peanut oil, curry powder, garlic, and ginger into pot. Set to STOVETOP HIGH. Cook uncovered 1 minute or until garlic is tender, stirring often. Stir in shrimp. Cook uncovered 4 minutes or until shrimp are cooked through, stirring occasionally. Serve shrimp on wooden picks with cilantro leaf on top.

NINJA SERVING TIP

Try another, more spicy version: Replace curry powder with red or green curry paste and cook according to the above directions.

 STOVETOP/STEAM OVEN

GARLIC LEMON STEAMED CLAMS

Onion, garlic, lemon and beer create a cooking liquid
to infuse clams with flavor as they steam. Serve as an
appetizer or even a simple meal.

PREP: 5 minutes • **COOK:** 20 minutes • **SERVINGS:** 4

Ingredients

2 tablespoons olive oil

1 small onion, chopped

¼ teaspoon salt

3 cloves garlic, minced

1 cup beer

1 lemon, sliced

2 tablespoons fresh chopped parsley

2 dozen clams, scrubbed

Directions

1. Pour oil into pot. Set to STOVETOP HIGH and heat oil. Add onion and salt to pot. Cook uncovered 6 minutes or until onions are tender, stirring occasionally. Add garlic. Cook uncovered 1 minute, stirring often.

2. Add beer, lemon, and parsley to pot. Place clams on roasting rack and place rack into pot. Set to OVEN 375°F for 15 minutes, checking after 10 minutes. Cover and cook until clams are cooked and shells open. Serve clams with broth mixture.

NINJA SERVING TIP

Serve this dish with crusty bread for soaking up all the delicious broth.

 STOVETOP

WILD MUSHROOM CROSTINI

Sautéing in the pot enhances the earthy flavor of the mushrooms, which are finished with Marsala wine and basil. Serve on crusty bread slices with a sprinkle of Parmesan cheese.

PREP: 10 minutes • **COOK:** 15 minutes • **SERVINGS:** 8

Ingredients

2 tablespoons butter

10 ounces assorted fresh wild mushrooms, sliced (cremini, shiitake, oyster, white)

2 shallots, minced

1 clove garlic, minced

½ teaspoon sea salt

⅛ teaspoon freshly ground black pepper

2 tablespoons Marsala wine

2 tablespoons finely chopped fresh basil leaves plus 16 small whole fresh basil leaves

16 slices (½-inch thick) French or Italian bread

2 tablespoons finely shredded Parmesan cheese

Directions

1. Place butter into pot. Set to STOVETOP HIGH and heat until butter is melted. Add mushrooms and shallots to pot. Cook uncovered 10 minutes or until mushrooms are lightly browned, stirring occasionally. Add garlic, salt, and black pepper. Cook 1 minute. Stir in wine. Cook 2 minutes or until wine is absorbed, stirring constantly. Stir in chopped basil.

2. Spoon **about 1 tablespoon** mushroom mixture onto each bread slice. Sprinkle with cheese and top each with 1 whole basil leaf.

NINJA TIME-SAVER TIP

Mushroom mixture can be made a day ahead and refrigerated. Simply reheat in pot on STOVETOP LOW, stirring occasionally, until hot.

 STOVETOP

PRETZEL-COATED CHICKEN TENDERS

This twist on chicken fingers features a crunchy pretzel coating and a decadent cheesy sauce for dipping. The chicken cooks up crisp on the outside and juicy on the inside, and you make the sauce in the pot, too! Only one pot to clean!

PREP: 10 minutes • **COOK:** 15 minutes • **SERVINGS:** 8

Ingredients

1 egg

2 cups butter-flavored pretzels, finely crushed

1 pound boneless chicken breast tenderloins

2 tablespoons vegetable oil

¾ cup beer or chicken broth

½ of a 16-ounce package pasteurized prepared cheese product, cut up

1 teaspoon Worcestershire sauce

1 teaspoon spicy brown mustard

Directions

1. Beat egg in shallow dish. Pour pretzel crumbs onto plate. Dip chicken into egg. Coat chicken with pretzel crumbs.

2. Pour oil into pot. Set to STOVETOP HIGH and heat oil. Add chicken to pot. Cook uncovered 10 minutes or until chicken is browned on both sides and cooked through. Remove chicken from pot, lightly cover, and keep warm.

3. Pour beer into pot and heat to a boil. Add cheese, Worcestershire sauce, and mustard. Cook uncovered until cheese is melted and mixture is smooth, stirring often. Serve sauce with chicken.

 **NINJA** SERVING TIP

Try cutting the chicken into bite-sized pieces before coating and cooking, then serve on a platter with wooden picks.

91

WHITE TURKEY CHILI

CHAPTER 4:
Soups/ Stews

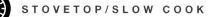 STOVETOP/SLOW COOK

BUTTERNUT SQUASH & APPLE SOUP

This soup tastes decadent but is packed with nutrients and fiber. Using a hand blender or immersion blender for the last step keeps it all in one pot!

PREP: 15 minutes • **COOK:** 1 hour, 10 minutes • **SERVINGS:** 6

Ingredients

2 tablespoons butter

1 package (20 ounces) fresh peeled cubed butternut squash (about 4 cups)

1 large onion, chopped

1 large Granny Smith apple, peeled, cored, and chopped

¼ teaspoon pumpkin pie spice or ground cinnamon

1 teaspoon salt

¼ teaspoon ground black pepper

3 cups chicken broth

2 bay leaves

¼ cup half-and-half

Directions

1. Place butter, squash, onion, and apple into pot. Set to STOVETOP HIGH. Cook uncovered 10 minutes or until squash is lightly browned, stirring occasionally. Stir in pumpkin pie spice, salt, and black pepper.

2. Add broth and bay leaves. Set to SLOW COOK HIGH for 1 to 2 hours. Cover and cook until squash is tender.

3. Remove and discard bay leaves. Make sure soup is cooled, and pour soup in batches to blender, making sure the jar is 2/3 full at a time. Puree soup mixture using a blender until smooth. Pour soup back in pot. Stir in half and half. Set to STOVETOP MED. Cook uncovered 5 minutes or until soup is hot.

> **NINJA** SERVING TIP
>
> Top each serving with sautéed fresh sage leaves: Heat 1 tablespoon olive oil in skillet over medium-high heat. Add ¼ cup fresh sage leaves. Cook 1 minute, turning once. Carefully remove leaves and drain on paper towels.

STOVETOP/SLOW COOK

CELERY & SWEET POTATO SOUP WITH BARLEY

There's no need to precook the barley in this recipe. It cooks right in the flavorful broth! Chunks of sweet potato and tomato make this vegetarian soup hearty and delicious.

PREP: 20 minutes • **COOK:** 4 hours • **SERVINGS:** 6

Ingredients

1 tablespoon olive oil

4 stalks celery, coarsely chopped

1 large onion, coarsely chopped

3 cloves garlic, minced

2 medium sweet potatoes, peeled and diced

1 teaspoon dried oregano leaves, crushed

½ teaspoon dried basil leaves, crushed

¼ teaspoon ground black pepper

6 cups vegetable broth

1 can (14½ ounces) diced tomatoes, undrained

½ cup uncooked medium pearl barley

Directions

1. Pour oil into pot. Set to STOVETOP HIGH and heat oil. Add celery and onion to pot. Cook uncovered 10 minutes or until vegetables are tender-crisp, stirring occasionally. Stir in garlic. Cook uncovered 2 minutes, stirring often.

2. Stir in potatoes, oregano, basil, black pepper, broth, tomatoes, and barley. Set to SLOW COOK HIGH for 4 to 5 hours. Cover and cook until barley is tender.

NINJA SERVING TIP

For an easy flavor twist, add 1 small head fresh fennel, coarsely chopped, with onion and celery.

STOVETOP/SLOW COOK

CHILI WITH CORN BREAD CRUST

Spicy red chili with beans simmers in pot, then cornbread batter is spooned on top. The corn bread bakes right on top of the chili — this main dish and side dish in one is perfect for a cold winter night!

PREP: 20 minutes • **COOK:** 4 hours, 10 minutes • **SERVINGS:** 6

Ingredients

1 tablespoon vegetable oil

1½ pounds ground beef or turkey

1 large onion, diced

1 green pepper, diced

1 tablespoon chili powder

½ teaspoon ground cinnamon

1 can (28 ounces) diced tomatoes, undrained

1 can (about 15 ounces) kidney beans, rinsed and drained

1 tablespoon tomato paste

1 package (8.5 ounces) corn muffin mix

1 egg, beaten

⅓ cup milk

Directions

1. Pour oil into pot. Set to STOVETOP HIGH and heat oil. Add beef, onion, and pepper to pot. Cook uncovered 10 minutes or until beef is browned, stirring occasionally. Spoon off any fat. Add chili powder and cinnamon to pot. Cook 5 minutes, stirring occasionally.

2. Stir tomatoes, beans, and tomato paste in pot. Set to SLOW COOK HIGH for 4 to 5 hours. Cover and cook.

3. After 4½ hours cooking time, stir muffin mix, egg, and milk in bowl. Uncover pot and spoon batter over chili. Cover and cook 30 minutes or until corn bread is cooked through.

NINJA SERVING TIP

Serve with sour cream and shredded Cheddar cheese.

STOVETOP/SLOW COOK

BUFFALO CHILI

This recipe is a great way to start cooking with buffalo meat. It is generally lower in fat and cholesterol than beef, and can be substituted for beef in many recipes.

PREP: 10 minutes • **COOK:** 2 hours, 20 minutes • **SERVINGS:** 6

Ingredients

2 pounds ground buffalo or bison

1 medium onion, chopped

1 large green pepper, chopped

3 cloves garlic, finely chopped

2 tablespoons chili powder

4 teaspoons ground cumin

1½ teaspoons salt

1 can (28 ounces) crushed tomatoes

2 tablespoons tomato paste

3 tablespoons Worcestershire sauce

2 tablespoons red wine vinegar

2 cans (15 ounces each) dark red kidney beans, drained and rinsed

Directions

1. Place buffalo, onion, pepper, and garlic into pot. Set to STOVETOP HIGH. Cook uncovered 20 minutes or until buffalo is cooked through, stirring occasionally.

2. Stir in remaining ingredients. Set to SLOW COOK HIGH for 2 to 3 hours. Cover and cook.

NINJA SERVING TIP

Serve this chili topped with sour cream, avocado, chopped fresh cilantro, shredded Cheddar or Monterey Jack cheese, and/or diced red onions.

STOVETOP/SLOW COOK

RED LENTIL & LEMON SOUP

Lentils are a great source of fiber, so this soup is light-tasting but very hearty. The lemon adds a bright Mediterranean touch. Sautéing the aromatics in the pot first brings out their flavor and gives dimension to the soup.

PREP: 15 minutes • **COOK:** 5 hours, 10 minutes • **SERVINGS:** 4

Ingredients

1 tablespoon olive oil

4 medium carrots, peeled and chopped

1 medium onion, chopped

2 cloves garlic, minced

½ teaspoon salt

2 teaspoons ground cumin

1½ cups dried red lentils

6 cups vegetable broth or water

¼ cup lemon juice

Directions

1. Pour oil into pot. Set to STOVETOP HIGH and heat oil. Add carrots, onion, garlic, and salt to pot. Cook uncovered 5 minutes or until vegetables are tender, stirring occasionally. Stir in cumin.

2. Stir in lentils and broth and heat to a boil. Set to SLOW COOK LOW for 5 to 7 hours. Cover and cook until lentils are tender. Stir in lemon juice before serving.

NINJA HEALTHY TIP

Iron-rich spinach is a beautiful addition to this soup. Stir in 1 package (about 10 ounces) fresh baby spinach. Cook 5 minutes or just until spinach is wilted. Don't overcook or you'll lose the bright green color.

STOVETOP/SLOW COOK

CHICKEN TORTILLA SOUP

This flavorful soup yields hearty bowlfuls of shredded chicken, tomatoes, beans, corn, and tortilla strips. Browning the chicken, then slow simmering in the pot locks in the flavor.

PREP: 20 minutes • **COOK:** 2 hours, 5 minutes • **SERVINGS:** 8

Ingredients

1 tablespoon canola oil

1¼ pounds boneless, skinless chicken breast halves

1 medium onion, chopped

2 cloves garlic, chopped

¼ cup fresh cilantro leaves, chopped

2 cans (14.5 ounces each) diced tomatoes, undrained

2 cans (10 ounces each) enchilada sauce

1 can (14.5 ounces) low-sodium chicken broth

1 can (about 15 ounces) black beans, undrained

1 package (10 ounces) frozen corn, thawed

1 tablespoon each chili powder and ground cumin

5 corn tortillas (6-inch), cut into 3 x ½-inch strips

Directions

1. Pour oil into pot. Set to STOVETOP MED and heat oil. Add chicken to pot. Cook uncovered 5 minutes or until chicken is lightly browned on both sides.

2. Stir onion, garlic, cilantro, tomatoes, enchilada sauce, broth, beans, corn, chili powder, and cumin in pot. Set to SLOW COOK HIGH for 2 to 3 hours. Cover and cook until chicken is fork-tender.

3. Place chicken in large bowl. Using two forks, shred chicken. Place chicken back in pot with soup. Top soup with tortillas before serving.

NINJA SERVING TIP

This soup is delicious served with diced avocado sprinkled on top with the tortillas.

STOVETOP/SLOW COOK

CREAMY CORN CHOWDER

Consistent heat from our pot makes from-scratch sauces simple. Add potatoes, corn, and broth and it's hands-free slow cooking to the finish.

PREP: 10 minutes • **COOK:** 4 hours, 5 minutes • **SERVINGS:** 6

Ingredients

2 tablespoons olive oil

1 medium onion, chopped

2 cloves garlic, chopped

8 ounces thick-sliced ham, cut into ¼-inch pieces

3 tablespoons all-purpose flour

1 large unpeeled russet potato, cut into ½-inch pieces

1 package (12 ounces) frozen corn, thawed

4 cups chicken broth

1 cup heavy cream

Oyster crackers

Directions

1. Place oil, onion, garlic, and ham in pot. Set to STOVETOP HIGH. Cook uncovered 3 minutes or until onion is tender, stirring occasionally. Stir in flour. Cook uncovered 1 minute, stirring constantly.

2. Add potato, corn, and broth to pot. Set to SLOW COOK HIGH for 4 to 5 hours. Cover and cook until potato is tender. Stir in cream and serve with crackers.

 **NINJA** TIME-SAVER TIP

Substitute 8 ounces chopped, cooked bacon for ham.

 **STOVETOP/SLOW COOK**

FRENCH ONION SOUP

Simple ingredients meet to make a sublime version of this classic soup. Onions are caramelized right in the pot, then finished on slow cook in the herb brandy broth until silky.

PREP: 10 minutes • **COOK:** 1 hour, 16 minutes • **SERVINGS:** 4

Ingredients

¼ **cup butter**

2 large onions, thinly sliced

6 sprigs fresh thyme

1½ **tablespoons chopped fresh rosemary leaves**

Salt and ground black pepper

¾ **cup brandy**

¼ **cup all-purpose flour**

1 package (32 ounces) beef stock

12 oven-baked garlic Italian toasts

½ **pound shredded Gruyère cheese**

Directions

1. Place butter into pot. Set to STOVETOP HIGH. Heat uncovered until butter is melted. Add onions, thyme, rosemary, salt, and black pepper. Cook uncovered 15 minutes or until onions are very tender, stirring occasionally. Stir in brandy and flour. Cook uncovered 1 minute or until mixture is thickened, stirring constantly.

2. Pour stock into pot. Season with salt and black pepper. Set to SLOW COOK HIGH for 1 to 2 hours. Cover and cook.

3. Place 3 toasts in each of 4 bowls. Sprinkle with cheese. Spoon soup over cheese-topped toasts.

NINJA SERVING TIP

If you can't find Italian toasts, use garlic or other purchased croutons.

STOVETOP/SLOW COOK

HEARTY BEEF STEW

Why brown and braise the beef in the same pot? You keep all the rich flavor of the browning, and it makes cleanup a breeze. This recipe adds the convenience of the slow cooker — no tending needed!

PREP: 10 minutes • **COOK:** 7 hours, 10 minutes • **SERVINGS:** 8

Ingredients

2 pounds beef for stew

1 teaspoon salt

½ teaspoon ground black pepper

¼ cup all-purpose flour

2 tablespoons vegetable oil

1½ cups beef broth

4 red potatoes, cut in half

2 onions, cut in quarters

1 cup baby carrots

4 cloves garlic, chopped

2 sprigs fresh thyme or 1 teaspoon dried thyme leaves, crushed

1 cup frozen peas, thawed

Directions

1. Season beef with salt and black pepper. Coat with flour.

2. Pour oil into pot. Set to STOVETOP HIGH and heat oil. Add beef and cook uncovered 10 minutes or until browned, stirring occasionally.

3. Stir broth, potatoes, onions, carrots, garlic, and thyme in pot. Set to SLOW COOK LOW for 7–9 hours. Cover and cook until beef is fork-tender. Stir in peas during last 10 minutes of cooking time.

NINJA TIME-SAVER TIP

You can reduce the SLOW COOK time by slow cooking on HIGH for 4 hours.

STOVETOP/SLOW COOK

CAULIFLOWER SOUP

Sauté cauliflower, make homemade cream sauce, then simmer to perfection, all in one pot! You can make a special soup like this one anytime when it's this easy.

PREP: 10 minutes • **COOK:** 2 hours, 20 minutes • **SERVINGS:** 4

Ingredients

1 tablespoon olive oil

1 head cauliflower (about 1½ pounds), trimmed and cut into florets

1 small onion, chopped

2 small cloves garlic, minced

2 tablespoons butter, melted

2 tablespoons all-purpose flour

1 teaspoon salt

¼ teaspoon ground black pepper

¼ teaspoon ground nutmeg

1 carton (32 ounces) vegetable broth

Directions

1. Pour oil into pot. Set to STOVETOP HIGH and heat oil. Add cauliflower, onion, and garlic to pot and toss to coat. Cook uncovered 5 minutes or until cauliflower is browned, stirring occasionally.

2. Stir butter, flour, salt, black pepper, and nutmeg into pot. Cook uncovered 2 minutes, stirring constantly. Stir in 2 cups broth. Cover and cook 5 minutes or until mixture boils and thickens. Stir in remaining broth. Set to SLOW COOK HIGH for 2 to 3 hours. Cover and cook until cauliflower is tender.

3. Puree soup mixture using a blender until smooth. Make sure soup is cooled, and pour soup in batches to blender, making sure the jar is 2/3 full at a time. Place soup back to pot. Set to STOVETOP MED. Cook uncovered 5 minutes or until soup is hot.

NINJA SERVING TIP

Add croutons and a thinly sliced cauliflower floret for a pretty garnish for this soup.

STOVETOP/SLOW COOK

SMOKY NEW ENGLAND CLAM CHOWDER

Poach clams and make homemade clam broth then move along to slow cook this hearty chowder all in the same pot!

PREP: 15 minutes • **COOK:** 2 hours • **SERVINGS:** 6

Ingredients

3 cups chicken broth

3 dozen littleneck clams, scrubbed

4 slices bacon

2 pounds white potatoes, peeled and cut into cubes

1 large sweet onion, chopped

2 stalks celery, thinly sliced

2 tablespoons all-purpose flour

2 small bay leaves

1 cup light cream

1 teaspoon salt

¼ teaspoon white pepper

2 tablespoons finely chopped parsley

Directions

1. Add **1 cup** chicken broth and clams to pot. Set to STOVETOP HIGH. Cover and cook 10 minutes or until clams are cooked. Remove clams and broth. Remove clams from shells, reserving 8 for garnish. Refrigerate clams. Strain broth mixture and reserve.

2. Add bacon to pot. Set to STOVETOP HIGH. Cook uncovered 10 minutes or until bacon is crisp, stirring occasionally. Drain bacon on paper towels and crumble.

3. Add potatoes, onion, and celery to pot. Set to STOVETOP HIGH. Cook uncovered 10 minutes or until tender, stirring occasionally. Stir in flour. Cook uncovered 2 minutes, stirring often. Stir in remaining chicken broth, reserved broth mixture, and bay leaves. Set to SLOW COOK HIGH for 1 to 2 hours. Cover and cook.

4. Discard bay leaves. Lightly mash potatoes in soup. Stir in reserved clams, cream, salt, and pepper. Set to SLOW COOK HIGH for 30 minutes. Cover and cook until soup is hot. Stir in parsley. Top each serving with clam in shell, bacon, and parsley.

NINJA HEALTHY TIP

Substitute fat-free low-sodium chicken broth for regular broth and fat-free half-and-half for light cream.

STOVETOP/SLOW COOK

POTATO LEEK SOUP WITH GARLIC CROUTONS & GORGONZOLA

Sautéing leeks and garlic first brings out their sweetness, which then complements the richness of Gorgonzola in this recipe.

PREP: 10 minutes • **COOK:** 1 hour, 10 minutes • **SERVINGS:** 4

Ingredients

¼ cup butter

2 leeks, chopped

3 cloves garlic, minced

Salt and ground black pepper

2 russet potatoes, peeled and cut into ½-inch pieces

1 package (32 ounces) chicken stock

Garlic croutons

4 tablespoons crumbled Gorgonzola cheese

Directions

1. Place butter into pot. Set to STOVETOP HIGH and heat uncovered until butter is melted. Stir in leeks and garlic. Season with salt and black pepper. Cook 10 minutes or until leeks are very tender, stirring occasionally.

2. Stir in potatoes and chicken stock. Set to SLOW COOK HIGH for 1 to 2 hours. Cover and cook until potatoes are tender. Puree soup mixture using a blender until smooth. Make sure soup is cooled, and pour soup in batches to blender, making sure the jar is 2/3 full at a time. Place soup back to pot. Set to STOVETOP MED. Cook uncovered 5 minutes or until soup is hot. Season with salt and black pepper.

3. Serve soup topped with croutons and Gorgonzola.

NINJA SERVING TIP

Instead of garnishing with Gorgonzola, add it to hot soup and blend until smooth.

 **STOVETOP/SLOW COOK**

HEARTY SEAFOOD STEW

Enjoy the savory slow-cooked broth of tomatoes, wine, fennel, and onion for dipping crusty, warm Italian bread with your meal.

PREP: 15 minutes • **COOK:** 4 hours • **SERVINGS:** 6

Ingredients

2 tablespoons olive oil

1 medium onion, chopped

1 bulb fennel, thinly sliced crosswise

1 clove garlic, chopped

½ teaspoon crushed red pepper

1 cup dry white wine

1 can (14.5 ounces) diced tomatoes, undrained

½ pound large sea scallops

¾ pound cod fillets, cut into 1-inch pieces

½ pound uncooked jumbo shrimp, peeled and deveined

2 pounds mussels, scrubbed

1 loaf crusty Italian bread, sliced and toasted

Directions

1. Add oil, onion, fennel, garlic, and red pepper to pot. Set to STOVETOP HIGH. Cook uncovered 3 minutes or until onions are tender, stirring occasionally.

2. Stir in wine and tomatoes. Cover and set to SLOW COOK HIGH for 3–4 hours. After 3½ hours, add seafood and cook for 20–30 minutes or until mussels open and seafood is cooked through. Discard mussels that do not open. Serve with bread.

NINJA SERVING TIP

To toast bread, brush bread slices on both sides with olive oil, season with salt and pepper, and place on baking sheet. Bake at 400°F 10 to 15 minutes or until golden.

 STOVETOP/SLOW COOK

WHITE TURKEY CHILI

Browning turkey and sausage adds an extra dimension of flavor to this wholesome chili — and there's no extra skillet to clean!

PREP: 30 minutes • **COOK:** 7 hours • **SERVINGS:** 8

Ingredients

- 1 can (7 ounces) chipotle peppers in adobo sauce
- 2 tablespoons olive oil
- 1 pound ground turkey or chicken
- 1 pound Italian-style turkey sausage, casing removed
- 1 small white onion, diced
- 1 can (4.25 ounces) diced green chiles
- 2 cans (15.5 ounces each) cannellini beans, drained and rinsed
- 2½ cups chicken stock
- 1 clove garlic, chopped
- ½ teaspoon cayenne pepper
- 2 tablespoons chili powder
- 1½ teaspoons ground cumin
- ½ cup frozen corn

Directions

1. Finely chop **half** of the chipotle pepper and reserve **1 teaspoon** adobo sauce.

2. Pour **1 tablespoon** oil into pot. Set to STOVETOP HIGH and heat oil. Add turkey to pot. Cook uncovered until turkey is browned, stirring often. Add sausage and remaining oil to pot. Cook uncovered until sausage is browned, stirring often.

3. Stir chipotle pepper, reserved adobo sauce, onion, green chiles, beans, stock, garlic, cayenne pepper, chili powder, and cumin into pot. Set to SLOW COOK LOW for 7 to 9 hours. Cover and cook, stirring in corn during last 30 minutes of cooking time.

NINJA SERVING TIP

Top with a lime crema (sour cream and lime juice), diced avocado, diced red or yellow peppers, or cilantro as desired.

STOVETOP/SLOW COOK

THAI-STYLE PORK STEW

An inexpensive cut of pork and ingredients from your pantry become a special-occasion dish with very little effort. Choose the time that works best for you — either 4 hours on HIGH or 7 hours on LOW.

PREP: 10 minutes • **COOK:** 4 hours, 10 minutes • **SERVINGS:** 6

Ingredients

1 boneless pork shoulder roast (2½ to 3 pounds)

Salt and ground black pepper

1 tablespoon vegetable oil

2 medium red peppers, cut into 1-inch pieces

6 green onions, cut into 1½-inch pieces

3 cloves garlic, minced

⅛ cup each teriyaki sauce and rice wine vinegar

1 tablespoon hot pepper sauce

⅓ cup creamy peanut butter

Hot cooked basmati rice

½ cup dry roasted peanuts

Directions

1. Season pork with salt and black pepper.

2. Pour oil into pot. Set to STOVETOP HIGH and heat oil. Place pork into pot. Cook uncovered 15 minutes or until pork is browned on all sides. Add peppers, half of green onions, garlic, teriyaki sauce, vinegar, and pepper sauce. Set to SLOW COOK HIGH for 4 to 5 hours. Cover and cook until pork is tender.

3. Remove pork to cutting board and cut into 1-inch pieces. Stir peanut butter into pot. Return pork to pot. Serve pork mixture over rice. Sprinkle with remaining onions and peanuts.

NINJA SERVING TIP

Toss some chopped fresh parsley into cooked rice.

CHICKEN MATZO BALL SOUP

Poaching chicken in the pot keeps texture consistently tender. Turn to slow cook to finish the soup — even the matzo balls — they cook right in the soup!

PREP: 20 minutes • **COOK:** 1 hour, 45 minutes • **SERVINGS:** 6

Ingredients

½ cup matzo meal

2 large eggs

¼ cup vegetable oil or melted butter

2 tablespoons water

1½ teaspoons salt

¾ teaspoon ground black pepper

6 cups chicken broth

1 pound skinless, boneless chicken breast halves

2 carrots, peeled and chopped

1 medium onion, chopped

3 stalks celery, thinly sliced

2 small bay leaves

2 tablespoons chopped fresh parsley

Directions

1. Stir matzo meal, eggs, oil, water, **½ teaspoon** salt, and **½ teaspoon** black pepper in bowl. Cover and refrigerate.

2. Pour **1 cup** broth into pot and add chicken. Set to STOVETOP HIGH. Cover and cook 15 minutes or until chicken is cooked through. Remove chicken from pot. Using 2 forks, shred chicken.

3. Add remaining broth, carrots, onion, celery, bay leaves, shredded chicken, and remaining salt and black pepper to pot. Set to SLOW COOK HIGH for 1 to 2 hours. Cover and cook.

4. Drop rounded tablespoons of matzo mixture into soup. **Do not stir.** Set to SLOW COOK HIGH for 30 minutes. Cover and cook until matzo balls are cooked through. Sprinkle with parsley.

NINJA SERVING TIP

For the perfect main-dish meal, serve with a simple salad. For fluffier matzo balls, try substituting plain seltzer for water.

STOVETOP/SLOW COOK

SAUSAGE, CHICKEN, & SHRIMP GUMBO

An important component of making gumbo is the roux, a mixture of flour and oil used to thicken and provide a perfect rich brown color, thanks to the even heat surrounding our pot.

PREP: 15 minutes • **COOK:** 7 hours, 30 minutes • **SERVINGS:** 6

Ingredients

½ cup plus 1 tablespoon vegetable oil

¾ pound smoked sausage, sliced

¾ pound boneless, skinless chicken thighs, cut into 2-inch pieces

⅔ cup flour

1 large onion, chopped

1 medium green pepper, chopped

3 stalks celery, chopped

2 cloves garlic, minced

3 cups chicken broth

1 can (14.5 ounces) diced tomatoes

½ teaspoon dried thyme leaves, crushed

¾ pound uncooked large shrimp, peeled and deveined

Directions

1. Pour **1 tablespoon** oil into pot. Set to STOVETOP HIGH and heat oil. Add sausage and chicken. Cook uncovered 10 minutes or until browned, stirring occasionally. Remove sausage and chicken from pot.

2. Stir in remaining oil and flour. Set to STOVETOP MED. Cook uncovered 7 minutes or until flour mixture turns deep brown, stirring constantly with a wooden spoon.

3. Add onion, pepper, celery, and garlic. Cook uncovered 5 minutes or until tender. Stir in broth, tomatoes, and thyme and heat to a boil. Set to SLOW COOK LOW for 7 to 9 hours. Cover and cook.

4. Stir in shrimp. Set to SLOW COOK HIGH for 15 minutes. Cover and cook until shrimp are cooked through.

NINJA SERVING TIP

If you like gumbo with some heat, simply stir in ¼ to ½ teaspoon cayenne pepper with the broth mixture. This recipe is even better when made the day before serving.

CHICKEN SOUP WITH BARLEY & SPINACH

Fresh good-for-you vegetables added to rotisserie chicken, seasoned broth, and barley make for hearty homemade goodness.

PREP: 20 minutes • **COOK:** 2 hours, 10 minutes • **SERVINGS:** 8

Ingredients

2 tablespoons olive or vegetable oil

2 carrots, peeled and chopped

2 cups sliced assorted mushrooms

1 large onion, chopped

2 stalks celery, thinly sliced

1 teaspoon salt

½ teaspoon ground black pepper

6 cups chicken broth

1 cup uncooked pearl barley

2 small bay leaves

1 can (14.5 ounces) diced tomatoes, undrained

1 bag (6 ounces) fresh baby spinach

1 rotisserie chicken, removed from bone and shredded

Directions

1. Add oil, carrots, mushrooms, onion, and celery to pot. Set to STOVETOP HIGH. Cook uncovered 10 minutes or until vegetables are lightly browned, stirring occasionally. Season with salt and black pepper.

2. Stir in broth, barley, and bay leaves. Set to SLOW COOK HIGH for 2 to 3 hours. Cover and cook, stirring in tomatoes, spinach and chicken for last 30 minutes of cooking time. Remove and discard bay leaves before serving.

NINJA HEALTHY TIP

This soup makes a terrific dinner. Serve with melon slices and crusty French bread.

PRIME RIB AU JUS

CHAPTER 5:
Entrees

Signature

BALSAMIC GLAZED CHICKEN WITH RADICCHIO

Cooking the radicchio enhances its slightly bitter flavor, which balances beautifully with this savory sauce. Browning the chicken in the pot first is essential to creating a rich flavor base — and the radicchio cooks in the same pot, so no extra saucepans to clean.

PREP: 10 minutes • **COOK:** 50 minutes • **SERVINGS:** 4

Ingredients

2 cloves garlic, minced

4 tablespoons chopped fresh rosemary leaves

Salt and ground black pepper

4 tablespoons olive oil

4 bone-in chicken breasts (about 2 pounds)

1 large red onion, thickly sliced

¾ cup red wine

½ cup balsamic vinegar

¼ cup water

2 heads radicchio, cut in quarters, keeping stem intact

Directions

1. Stir garlic, rosemary, salt, black pepper, and **3 tablespoons** olive oil in bowl. Rub chicken with garlic mixture. Let stand 20 minutes.

2. Place chicken into pot, skin side down. Set to STOVETOP HIGH. Cook uncovered 5 minutes or until browned. Remove chicken from pot.

3. Add onion to pot. Place roasting rack into pot and place chicken on rack. Pour wine, vinegar, and water over chicken. Set OVEN to 375°F for 40 minutes. Cover and cook until chicken is cooked through.

4. Remove chicken from pot, cover, and keep warm. Add radicchio to onion mixture. Cover and cook 4 minutes or until radicchio is tender. Serve sauce and radicchio over chicken.

NINJA SERVING TIP

Serve with smashed potatoes or with crusty bread to soak up the delicious sauce.

 STEAM OVEN

PROVENCE CHICKEN,

Chicken is rubbed with a flavorful mixture of herbs, garlic, shallot and Dijon mustard, then browned in the pot to seal in the juices. Steam roasting to finish keeps meat moist and tender.

PREP: 10 minutes • **COOK:** 1 hour, 15 minutes • **SERVINGS:** 6

Ingredients

- 1 small bunch fresh parsley, chopped
- 2 garlic cloves, coarsely chopped
- 1 large shallot, coarsely chopped
- 1 tablespoon herbes de Provence
- 1 sprig fresh rosemary, stem removed
- 1½ tablespoons Dijon-style mustard
- 1 teaspoon kosher salt
- 1 teaspoon ground black pepper
- 3 tablespoons olive oil
- Grated zest of 1 lemon
- 6 pound whole roasting chicken giblets and neck removed
- 4 cups water or chicken broth

Directions

1. Add parsley, garlic, shallot, herbes de Provence, rosemary, mustard, salt, and black pepper to food processor. Cover and pulse until mixture is finely chopped. With processor running, slowly add 3 tablespoons olive oil. Continue processing until smooth paste forms. Add lemon zest and pulse.

2. Rub parsley mixture on chicken, on all sides, under skin, and inside cavity. Set to STOVETOP HIGH and add chicken to pot. Cook 15 minutes or until chicken is browned on all sides. Remove chicken from pot.

3. Pour water into pot. Place chicken on roasting rack and place rack into pot. Set OVEN to 350°F for 1 hour, 15 minutes. Cover and cook until chicken is cooked through.

NINJA SERVING TIP

Serve with mashed potatoes and oven-browned carrots.

STOVETOP/STEAM OVEN

ROAST BEEF WITH GARLIC MUSTARD CRUST

You won't need a separate skillet and roasting pan to make this restaurant-worthy dish. A crisp, flavorful crust surrounds juicy, tender perfectly cooked beef.

PREP: 10 minutes • **COOK:** 1 hour, 5 minutes • **SERVINGS:** 8

Ingredients

6 tablespoons butter

3 cloves garlic, finely chopped

1½ cups Japanese-style bread crumbs (panko)

3 tablespoons finely chopped fresh parsley

Salt and ground black pepper

1 beef eye round roast (2½ to 3 pounds)

1½ tablespoons olive oil

3 cups beef broth

2 tablespoons Dijon-style mustard

Directions

1. Stir **3 tablespoons** butter, garlic, bread crumbs, and parsley in bowl. Season with salt and black pepper.

2. Place remaining butter into pot. Set to STOVETOP HIGH and heat until butter is melted. Add bread crumb mixture to pot. Cook uncovered 2 minutes or until bread crumb mixture is lightly browned, stirring occasionally. Remove bread crumb mixture from pot.

3. Season beef with salt and black pepper.

4. Pour oil into pot. Set to STOVETOP HIGH and heat oil. Add beef to pot. Cook uncovered 15 minutes or until beef is browned on all sides. Remove beef from pot.

5. Pour broth into pot. Place roasting rack into pot. Place beef on rack. Set OVEN to 375°F for 45 minutes. Cover and cook 45 minutes for medium-well or until desired doneness.

6. Spread mustard on beef and coat with bread crumb mixture.

NINJA SERVING TIP

Serve with roasted red potatoes with rosemary.

STOVETOP/STEAM OVEN

Signature

COFFEE-BRAISED BEEF WITH MUSHROOM SAUCE

The caramelized flavor from browning the beef in the pot is enhanced by the roasted notes in the coffee. Covered cooking to finish keeps the meat moist and tender.

PREP: 10 minutes • **COOK:** 1 hour, 40 minutes • **SERVINGS:** 8

Ingredients

- 1 boneless beef rump roast (about 3 pounds)
- 1 teaspoon salt
- ½ teaspoon ground black pepper
- 2 tablespoons butter
- 2 tablespoons olive oil
- 1 package (8 ounces) sliced baby portobello mushrooms
- 1 large onion, chopped
- 4 cloves garlic, minced
- 2 cups strong-brewed black coffee
- ¼ cup red wine vinegar
- ¼ cup all-purpose flour
- ¼ cup cold water

Directions

1. Season beef with salt and black pepper.

2. Place butter and oil into pot. Set to STOVETOP HIGH and heat until butter is melted. Add beef to pot. Cook uncovered 15 minutes or until beef is browned on all sides. Remove beef from pot.

3. Add mushrooms and onion to pot. Cook uncovered 15 minutes or until vegetables are tender-crisp, stirring occasionally. Stir in garlic. Cook 2 minutes, stirring constantly. Stir in coffee and vinegar.

4. Place beef on roasting rack. Place rack into pot. Set OVEN to 375°F for 55 minutes. Cover and cook 55 minutes for medium or until desired doneness. Remove rack and beef from pot. Cover beef and keep warm.

5. Stir flour and ¼ cup water in bowl until smooth. Stir flour mixture and remaining water into pot. Set to STOVETOP HIGH. Cook uncovered 10 minutes or until mixture boils and thickens, stirring often. Serve beef with mushroom sauce.

NINJA HEALTHY TIP

Serve with buttermilk smashed red potatoes and a green salad.

STOVETOP/SLOW COOK

Signature

SAVORY POT ROAST

This recipe elevates an inexpensive cut of meat to something worthy of a special meal. Browning beef first is essential to creating the rich flavor base, and now you can do it all in the same pot.

PREP: 20 minutes • **COOK:** 6 hours, 25 minutes • **SERVINGS:** 8

Ingredients

1 boneless beef chuck roast (3 to 4 pounds)

¼ cup plus 2 tablespoons flour

¼ cup olive oil

2 carrots, peeled and chopped

2 stalks celery, chopped

1 medium onion, chopped

3 cloves garlic, crushed

1 can (28 ounces) whole plum tomatoes in purée

1 cup each red wine and beef broth

3 sprigs fresh thyme

2 sprigs fresh rosemary

1 tablespoon butter, softened

Directions

1. Coat beef with ¼ **cup** flour.

2. Pour **half** of oil into pot. Set to STOVETOP HIGH and heat oil. Add beef to pot. Cook uncovered 10 minutes or until browned on all sides. Remove beef from pot.

3. Add remaining oil, carrots, celery, onion, and garlic to pot. Cook uncovered 10 minutes or until vegetables are tender, stirring occasionally. Add tomatoes, wine, broth, thyme, and rosemary and heat to a boil.

4. Return beef to pot. Set to SLOW COOK LOW for 6 to 8 hours. Cover and cook until beef is fork-tender.

5. Remove beef to cutting board. Stir butter and remaining flour in bowl. Stir butter mixture into pot. Set to STOVETOP HIGH. Cook uncovered 2 minutes or until gravy is thickened. Serve beef with gravy.

NINJA TIME-SAVER TIP

Cook pot roast in about half the time: Set pot to SLOW COOK HIGH for 4 to 5 hours.

SWEET & SPICY PORK BABY BACK RIBS

Browning the ribs in the pot seals in the flavor of the smoky-sweet spice rub, then steam roasting cooks the ribs until the meat is falling off the bone. Glazing with barbeque sauce to finish adds an extra layer of flavor.

PREP: 10 minutes • **COOK:** 1 hour, 15 minutes • **SERVINGS:** 4

Ingredients

1 tablespoon smoked paprika

1 tablespoon packed brown sugar

⅛ teaspoon cayenne pepper

1 rack pork baby back ribs (about 3 pounds), cut in half

Salt and ground black pepper

1 tablespoon vegetable oil

3 cups beef broth or water

½ cup barbeque sauce

Directions

1. Stir paprika, brown sugar, and cayenne pepper in bowl. Rub ribs with paprika mixture. Season with salt and black pepper.

2. Pour oil into pot. Set to STOVETOP HIGH and heat oil. Add **half** the ribs to pot. Cook uncovered 5 minutes or until browned on both sides. Remove ribs from pot. Repeat with remaining ribs. Remove ribs from pot.

3. Pour broth into pot. Place roasting rack into pot. Place ribs on rack. Set OVEN to 375°F for 1 hour. Cover and cook until pork is fork-tender.

4. Uncover pot and brush ribs with sauce. Set OVEN to 375°F for 10 minutes. Cover and cook until sauce is hot.

NINJA SERVING TIP

After cooking, cut ribs in between bones for easy serving.

STOVETOP/STEAM OVEN

Signature

PRIME RIB AU JUS

Searing the beef in the pot first ensures a flavorful crust that tastes great and helps to seal in the juices. Finish cooking the beef, then use the drippings to create a rich, meaty au jus. A special-occasion main dish, and only one pot to clean!

PREP: 10 minutes • **COOK:** 1 hour, 30 minutes • **SERVINGS:** 4

Ingredients

1 beef standing rib roast
(about 5 pounds)

Salt and ground black pepper

1 tablespoon chopped fresh
rosemary leaves

4 cups beef broth

1 tablespoon butter, softened

1 tablespoon all-purpose flour

Directions

1. Season beef with salt, black pepper, and rosemary. Set pot to STOVETOP HIGH and heat pan. Add beef and cook uncovered 10 minutes or until browned on all sides. Remove beef from pot.

2. Pour broth into pot. Place roasting rack into pot. Place beef on rack. Set OVEN to 350°F for 1 hour. Cover and cook 1 hour for medium-rare or until desired doneness. Remove beef to cutting board and cover with foil.

3. Stir butter and flour in bowl. Add butter mixture to pot. Set to STOVETOP HIGH. Cook 10 minutes or until mixture is slightly reduced, stirring constantly. Serve sauce with beef.

 SERVING TIP

Serve with garlic mashed potatoes and creamed spinach for a real steakhouse-style dinner!

 STOVETOP/SLOW COOK

PORK CHOPS PROVENÇAL

Provençal cooking brings the flavors of France and the Mediterranean together. Pork is simmered in a sauce rich with the flavors of vegetables, bacon, and fennel. Slow cooking melds the flavors for a perfectly seasoned dish.

PREP: 15 minutes • **COOK:** 5 hours, 25 minutes • **SERVINGS:** 6

Ingredients

¼ **pound bacon, cut into 1-inch strips**

6 **bone-in center-cut pork chops**

Salt and ground black pepper

1 **large onion, thinly sliced**

3 **cloves garlic, minced**

1 **can (14.5 ounces) chopped tomatoes, undrained**

1 **package (8 ounces) frozen artichoke hearts, thawed and drained**

1 **cup pitted kalamata olives**

1 **tablespoon fennel seeds**

Directions

1. Set to STOVETOP MED and place bacon in pot. Cook uncovered 10 minutes or until bacon is crisp, stirring occasionally. Remove bacon from pot and drain on paper towels.

2. Season pork with salt and black pepper. Add pork to pot. Cook 10 minutes or until browned on both sides.

3. Return bacon to pot. Add onion, garlic, tomatoes, artichokes, olives, and fennel seeds to pot. Cook 5 minutes, stirring occasionally. Set to SLOW COOK LOW for 5 to 7 hours. Cover and cook until pork is fork-tender.

NINJA HEALTHY TIP

To provide the same great flavor, substitute turkey bacon for the bacon in this recipe.

UPSIDE-DOWN MAC & CHEESE

A macaroni and cheese version of spaghetti pie, this recipe features cheese-sauced pasta baked in a Cheddar bread crumb crust. Everything is cooked in the same pot for easy cleanup.

PREP: 15 minutes • **COOK:** 20 minutes • **SERVINGS:** 8

Ingredients

4 cups water

1 pound uncooked elbow macaroni

¾ cup butter

6 tablespoons all-purpose flour

5 cups whole milk

6¾ cups shredded extra-sharp Cheddar cheese

½ cup grated Pecorino Romano or Parmesan cheese

Salt and ground black pepper

Cooking spray

1½ cups bread crumbs

Directions

1. Pour water into pot. Set to STOVETOP HIGH. Heat uncovered to a boil. Stir in macaroni. Cook uncovered 9 minutes or until macaroni is just tender, stirring occasionally. Remove macaroni from pot and drain well in colander, reserving **1 cup** cooking water.

2. Add ½ cup butter to pot. Set to STOVETOP MED and heat until butter is melted. Stir in flour. Cook uncovered 3 minutes, stirring constantly. Add milk and heat to a boil, stirring constantly. Cook uncovered 3 minutes, or until mixture is thickened and smooth, stirring occasionally. Stir in **6 cups** Cheddar cheese, ¼ cup Pecorino Romano cheese, salt, and pepper until cheeses are melted, stirring occasionally. Turn off pot.

3. Stir cheese mixture, macaroni, and reserved cooking water in large bowl. Carefully remove pot and wipe dry, allowing it to cool before handling.

4. Melt remaining ¼ cup butter. Stir melted butter, bread crumbs, ¾ cup Cheddar cheese, and ¼ cup Pecorino Romano in bowl.

5. Spray pot with cooking spray. Press bread crumb mixture onto bottom and 1 inch up sides of pot. Pour in macaroni mixture. Set OVEN to 350°F for 20 minutes, checking after 15 minutes. Cook until golden brown on bottom and sides and invert onto plate.

NINJA HEALTHY TIP

Serve with sliced fresh tomato salad.

STOVETOP/SLOW COOK

MEDITERRANEAN CHICKEN WITH ARTICHOKES & COUSCOUS

Succulent chicken thighs brown in pot to anchor the flavor in this one-pot dish. Couscous cooks in flavorful cooking liquid at the end.

PREP: 15 minutes • **COOK:** 4 hours, 5 minutes • **SERVINGS:** 8

Ingredients

1 tablespoon olive oil

8 bone-in skinless chicken thighs

1 large onion, chopped

4 cloves garlic, chopped

1 can (28 ounces) crushed tomatoes

1 package (8 ounces) frozen artichokes, thawed and drained

1 tablespoon Italian seasoning, crushed

1 teaspoon salt

½ teaspoon ground black pepper

1 cup uncooked couscous

½ cup pitted ripe olives

Directions

1. Pour oil into pot. Set to STOVETOP HIGH and heat oil. Add chicken in batches to pot. Cook uncovered 5 minutes or until chicken is lightly browned.

2. Add onion, garlic, tomatoes, artichokes, Italian seasoning, salt, and black pepper to pot. Set to SLOW COOK HIGH for 4 to 5 hours. Cover and cook, stirring in couscous and olives during last 15 minutes of cooking time.

NINJA SERVING TIP

Sprinkle with toasted pine nuts before serving.

136

 OVEN

MOROCCAN SPICED CHICKEN THIGHS

Flavorful chicken thighs rubbed with perfectly balanced sweet and hot spice mixture stay moist and tender cooked in this covered pot.

PREP: 10 minutes • **COOK:** 40 minutes • **SERVINGS:** 6

Ingredients

- 1 tablespoon paprika
- 1 tablespoon packed light brown sugar
- 2 teaspoons ground cumin
- 1 teaspoon ground cinnamon
- 1 teaspoon ground ginger
- 1 teaspoon salt
- 1 teaspoon garlic powder
- ¼ teaspoon ground black pepper
- ¼ teaspoon ground cayenne pepper
- 6 bone-in chicken thighs (about 2½ pounds)

Directions

1. Stir paprika, brown sugar, cumin, cinnamon, ginger, salt, garlic powder, black pepper, and cayenne pepper in bowl. Rub seasoning mixture over chicken thighs, coating all sides and under skin.

2. Place roasting rack into pot and place chicken on rack. Set OVEN to 400°F for 40 minutes. Cover and cook until chicken is cooked through.

 **NINJA** SERVING TIP

Serve with couscous cooked in chicken broth, cumin, cinnamon, and ginger with added raisins and chopped green onions.

STOVETOP/STEAM OVEN

LEMON CHICKEN WITH ROSEMARY

Fresh lemon and rosemary complement the richly roasted flavor of the chicken, made moist and tender using this foolproof cooking method.

PREP: 15 minutes • **COOK:** 1 hour, 15 minutes • **SERVINGS:** 6

Ingredients

1 lemon

3 sprigs fresh rosemary

6 pound whole roasting chicken

Salt and ground black pepper

2 large onions, sliced

3 cloves garlic, sliced

4 cups chicken broth

Directions

1. Grate and reserve **1 tablespoon** zest from lemon. Cut lemon in quarters. Chop and reserve **1 sprig** rosemary.

2. Remove package of giblets and neck from chicken cavities. Rinse chicken and pat dry with paper towel. Place lemon quarters and remaining rosemary sprigs into chicken cavity. Season chicken with salt and pepper.

3. Set to STOVETOP HIGH. Place chicken into pot. Cook uncovered, searing chicken for approximately 5–7 minutes on each side as desired. Remove chicken from pot and place on roasting rack.

4. Place onions, garlic and broth into pot. Place rack with chicken in pot. Sprinkle chicken with reserved lemon zest and chopped rosemary. Set OVEN to 375°F for 1 hour and 15 minutes. Cover and cook until chicken is cooked through and juices run clear.

NINJA TIME-SAVER TIP

Use leftovers from this delicious chicken for two or more meals later in the week. Great for lunch with mixed salad greens, chopped fresh vegetables, and low-fat dressing.

Entrees

SICILIAN MEATLOAF

This meatloaf's savory meat and cheese flavors are balanced with the addition of sweet raisins. It's an unexpectedly addictive combination!

PREP: 5 minutes • **COOK:** 1 hour • **SERVINGS:** 6

Ingredients

1½ **pounds meatloaf mix (ground pork, beef, and veal)**

¾ **cup grated Pecorino Romano cheese**

½ **cup bread crumbs**

2 **eggs, lightly beaten**

½ **cup golden raisins**

1 ¼ **cups loosely packed chopped fresh parsley**

Directions

1. Mix thoroughly meatloaf mix, cheese, bread crumbs, eggs, raisins, and 1 cup parsley in bowl. Press meatloaf mixture into 9x5-inch loaf pan.

2. Place roasting rack into pot. Place pan on rack. Set OVEN to 400°F for 1 hour. Cover and cook until meatloaf is cooked through. Remove meatloaf from pan and sprinkle with remaining parsley.

NINJA SERVING TIP

For a special touch, add 3 chopped hard-cooked eggs in center of meatloaf before cooking.

 STOVETOP/SLOW COOK

PORK CARNITAS

Well-browned pork cooks to succulent tenderness in a mixture of onion, garlic, vinegar, and brown sugar. Browning the pork in the pot first gives it a flavorful start.

PREP: 10 minutes • **COOK:** 4 hours, 10 minutes • **SERVINGS:** 10

Ingredients

1 tablespoon olive oil

3 to 4 pounds boneless pork shoulder

1 medium onion, sliced

3 cloves garlic, minced

1 cup chicken broth

¾ cup cider vinegar

2 tablespoons packed brown sugar

2 tablespoons dried oregano leaves, crushed

20 corn tortillas

2 tomatoes, chopped

Directions

1. Pour oil into pot. Set to STOVETOP HIGH and heat oil. Add pork to pot. Cook uncovered 10 minutes until browned on all sides. Add onion and garlic to pot.

2. Stir broth, vinegar, brown sugar, and oregano in bowl. Pour broth mixture over pork in pot. Set to SLOW COOK HIGH for 4 to 5 hours. Cover and cook until pork is fork-tender. Transfer pork into large bowl. Using two forks, shred pork.

3. Place **about 1/3 cup** pork mixture on **each** tortilla. Fold tortillas over filling. Sprinkle with tomatoes.

 SERVING TIP

Flavorful enough to be served simply as shown above, you can also add your favorite taco toppings or use pork as a filling for burritos or enchiladas.

OVEN

CAJUN SPICE RUBBED COUNTRY-STYLE PORK RIBS

Three ingredients are all you need to make these mouth watering ribs. The pot surrounds the meat with even heat, yielding fork-tender pork every time.

PREP: 5 minutes • **COOK:** 2 hours • **SERVINGS:** 6

Ingredients

3 tablespoons Cajun seasoning

2 tablespoons packed light brown sugar

3 pounds bone-in country-style pork ribs

2 cups water

Directions

1. Stir Cajun seasoning and brown sugar in bowl. Rub pork with seasoning mixture.

2. Pour water into pot. Place roasting rack into pot. Place pork on roasting rack. Place rack into pot. Set OVEN to 375°F for 2 hours. Cover and cook until pork is fork-tender.

NINJA SERVING TIP

Serve with macaroni and cheese, sliced tomatoes, and watermelon slices for dessert.

Entrees

CLASSIC BRAISED BEEF BRISKET

Cooking the brisket directly in the steam roasting environment, coupled with the infused braising liquid, both tenderizes and flavors the meat as it cooks for a juicy, delicious special meal.

PREP: 5 minutes • **COOK:** 3 hours, 40 minutes • **SERVINGS:** 8

Ingredients

1 beef brisket (about 2 ½ pounds)

Salt and ground black pepper

2 tablespoons vegetable oil

1 medium onion, chopped

1 medium carrot, peeled and chopped

1 stalk celery, chopped

10 cloves of garlic, peeled

2 sprigs fresh thyme

1 bay leaf

4 cups warm water

4 cups beef stock

1 cup dry white wine

Directions

1. Season beef with salt and black pepper.

2. Pour oil into pot. Set to STOVETOP HIGH and heat oil. Add beef to pot. Cook uncovered 15 minutes or until beef is browned on both sides. Spoon off fat.

3. Place onion and carrot around beef. Set to STOVETOP HIGH for 15 minutes. Cook uncovered until vegetables are lightly browned.

4. Add celery, garlic, thyme, and bay leaf to pot. Pour in the water, beef stock and wine, enough to cover meat. Set to OVEN 300°F for 3 hours. Cover and cook until beef is fork-tender, turning the beef over once halfway through cooking time. Remove beef from pot, cover, and keep warm.

5. Set pot to STOVETOP MED. Cook uncovered 10 minutes or until liquid is slightly reduced, stirring in remaining water if needed. Strain liquid through sieve. Season with salt and black pepper and serve with beef.

Note: For larger brisket cuts, add enough liquid, equal parts water and broth to cover meat.

NINJA SERVING TIP

Serve brisket with mashed potatoes or crusty bread to savor the flavorful cooking liquid.

 **STOVETOP/OVEN**

VEGETARIAN STUFFED PEPPERS

Peppers stuffed with couscous, chickpeas, and zucchini cook in a chunky tomato-onion sauce. Sauté onion for the sauce, then bake peppers, all in one pot!

PREP: 20 minutes • **COOK:** 35 minutes • **SERVINGS:** 4

Ingredients

2 tablespoons olive oil

1 small onion, chopped

1 can (28 ounces) Italian-style diced tomatoes

1 cup vegetable broth

Salt and ground black pepper

2 cups cooked couscous

1 zucchini, chopped

1 can (about 15 ounces) chickpeas, drained and rinsed

1 tablespoon chopped garlic

1 teaspoon Italian seasoning

½ cup grated Parmesan cheese

4 large red, yellow, or green peppers, tops, seeds and membranes removed and discarded

Directions

1. Pour oil into pot. Set to STOVETOP MED and heat oil. Stir in onion. Cook uncovered 8 minutes or until onion is tender, stirring occasionally. Stir in tomatoes and broth and season with salt and black pepper.

2. Stir couscous, zucchini, chickpeas, garlic, seasoning, and **half** the cheese in bowl. Season with salt and black pepper. Spoon couscous mixture into peppers and sprinkle with remaining cheese.

3. Place filled peppers into pot. Set OVEN to 250°F for 20 minutes. Cover and cook until peppers are tender. Serve peppers with tomato sauce.

NINJA HEALTHY TIP

For a healthier version of this, simply omit the cheese.

STOVETOP/OVEN

DRY-RUBBED ROASTED TURKEY TENDERLOINS WITH SWEET CHILI

A spiced, sweet dry rub seasons the turkey before it's seared in the pot. It's pan-roasting, but with an all-in-one appliance that doesn't heat up your kitchen!

PREP: 10 minutes • **COOK:** 30 minutes • **SERVINGS:** 6

Ingredients

- 1 tablespoon sugar
- 1 teaspoon salt
- 1 teaspoon ground cinnamon
- 1 teaspoon garlic powder
- ½ teaspoon dried thyme leaves, crushed
- ¼ teaspoon ground cumin
- 1 package (24 ounces) boneless turkey breast tenderloins
- 2 tablespoons olive oil
- ⅓ cup sweet chili sauce
- 1 teaspoon Worcestershire sauce

Directions

1. Stir sugar, salt, cinnamon, garlic powder, thyme, and cumin in bowl. Brush turkey with **1 tablespoon** oil. Rub turkey with sugar mixture.

2. Pour remaining oil into pot. Set to STOVETOP HIGH and heat oil. Add turkey to pot. Cook uncovered 15 minutes or until browned on both sides. Remove turkey from pot.

3. Place roasting rack into pot. Place turkey on rack. Set OVEN to 350°F for 10 minutes, checking after 8 minutes. Cover and cook until turkey is cooked through. Remove turkey from pot and let stand 5 minutes before slicing.

4. Stir chili sauce and Worcestershire sauce in bowl. Serve chili sauce mixture with turkey.

NINJA SERVING TIP

Substitute chicken or pork tenderloins for turkey if desired.

STOVETOP

SHRIMP & BROCCOLI SAUTÉ

Skip the thawing step with this twist on traditional scampi. Frozen shrimp, broccoli, and peas cook quickly in a lemony sauce, then are tossed with pasta and sprinkled with crunchy pine nuts.

PREP: 20 minutes • **COOK:** 25 minutes • **SERVINGS:** 4

Ingredients

1 lemon

1 tablespoon olive oil

1 large onion, sliced

3 cloves garlic, minced

1 teaspoon salt

½ teaspoon ground black pepper

1 pound uncooked frozen jumbo shrimp, peeled and deveined (about 16 per pound)

1 pound broccoli, cut into thin spears or 1 package (16 ounces) frozen broccoli cuts

½ cup frozen peas

1 can (14.5 ounces) chicken broth

¼ teaspoon crushed red pepper

½ of a 1-pound package linguine pasta, cooked and drained

⅓ cup toasted pine nuts

Directions

1. Grate **1 teaspoon** zest from lemon.

2. Pour oil into pot. Set to STOVETOP HIGH and heat oil. Add onion to pot. Cook uncovered 5 minutes or until onion is tender, stirring occasionally. Add garlic, salt, black pepper, and shrimp to pot. Cook 2 minutes, stirring often.

3. Stir in broccoli, peas, broth, red pepper, and lemon zest and heat to a boil. Cook 5 minutes or until broccoli is tender-crisp and shrimp are cooked through, stirring occasionally. Serve shrimp mixture over pasta and sprinkle with pine nuts.

NINJA SERVING TIP

This brothy dish would also be delicious served over hot cooked white rice instead of pasta.

 STOVETOP

TUSCAN CHICKEN & BEANS

Chicken goes right from the freezer into the pot — no need to thaw! It cooks until tender in a creamy Italian-seasoned sauce with white beans and spinach.

PREP: 10 minutes • **COOK:** 30 minutes • **SERVINGS:** 4

Ingredients

1 tablespoon olive oil

1 medium onion, chopped

2 cloves garlic, chopped

1½ teaspoons Italian seasoning, crushed

1 can (14.5 ounces) diced tomatoes, undrained

1 can (10¾ ounces) condensed cream of chicken soup

1 can (about 15 ounces) cannellini beans, rinsed and drained

¼ teaspoon ground black pepper

4 frozen skinless, boneless thin-sliced chicken cutlets (about 1 pound)

2 cups chopped fresh spinach

Directions

1. Pour oil into pot. Set to STOVETOP HIGH and heat oil. Add onion, garlic, and Italian seasoning to pot. Cook 5 minutes or until onion is tender, stirring occasionally.

2. Stir tomatoes, soup, beans, and black pepper into pot and heat to a boil. Add frozen chicken to pot. Set to STOVETOP LOW. Cover and cook 20 minutes or until chicken is cooked through, stirring in spinach during last 5 minutes of cooking time.

 **NINJA** SERVING TIP

Sprinkle with Parmesan cheese before serving

OVEN

PANKO PARMESAN-CRUSTED TILAPIA

Fish goes right from the freezer to the pot, no need to waste time thawing! The efficient cooking process gives you a crunchy crust and tender, flaky fish in no time!

PREP: 5 minutes • **COOK:** 40 minutes • **SERVINGS:** 4

Ingredients

- ½ cup seasoned Japanese-style bread crumbs (panko)
- 2 tablespoons grated Parmesan cheese
- ¼ teaspoon paprika
- 1 package (12 ounces) frozen tilapia fillets (4 fillets)
- 2 tablespoons Dijon-style mustard

Directions

1. Stir bread crumbs, cheese, and paprika on plate.

2. Place unwrapped frozen fish into multi-purpose pan, overlapping edges slightly to fit. Brush frozen fish with mustard. Sprinkle with bread crumb mixture. Place pan into top of pot. Set OVEN to 425°F for 40 minutes. Cover and cook until fish flakes easily when tested with fork.

NINJA SERVING TIP

Serve this meal with a side of pasta or rice and green bean salad from the deli counter.

 **SLOW COOK**

CHEESY CHICKEN BURRITOS

Make these hearty burritos stuffed with chicken, beans, and cheese, and everything, even warming the tortillas, cooks in one pot! Slow cooking intensifies the flavors in the filling and keeps the chicken moist and tender.

PREP: 10 minutes • **COOK:** 2 hours, 5 minutes • **SERVINGS:** 8

Ingredients

2 cups cubed cooked chicken

1 jar (16 ounces) picante sauce

1 can (15 ounces) black beans, rinsed and drained

1 can (4 ounces) diced green chiles, drained

1 tablespoon chopped fresh cilantro leaves

1 cup shredded Mexican four-cheese blend

8 flour tortillas (8-inch)

Sour cream

Directions

1. Stir chicken, picante sauce, beans, chiles, and cilantro in pot. Set to SLOW COOK HIGH for 2 to 3 hours. Cover and cook until chicken is cooked through.

2. Sprinkle chicken mixture with cheese. Place 9x6-inch baking pan into top of pot. Place tortillas in pan. Cover and cook 5 minutes or until tortillas are warmed.

3. Spoon **about 1/3 cup** chicken mixture on **each** tortilla. Roll tortillas around filling. Serve with sour cream.

NINJA SERVING TIP

Having a party? Recipe can easily be doubled.

ITALIAN BRAISED SHORT RIBS

This is classic comfort food: tender beef ribs slow-cooked with pancetta and vegetables. Browning the beef in the pot saves on cleanup, and gives the dish its depth of flavor.

PREP: 20 minutes • **COOK:** 6 hours, 20 minutes • **SERVINGS:** 6

Ingredients

4 to 5 pounds beef short ribs

¼ cup all-purpose flour

2 tablespoons olive oil

2 ounces pancetta, chopped

1 large onion, chopped

2 carrots, peeled and chopped

4 cloves garlic, minced

2 teaspoons dried oregano leaves, crushed

½ teaspoon each crushed red pepper, dried rosemary leaves, and dried thyme leaves, crushed

2 tablespoons tomato paste

1 can (14.5 ounces) diced tomatoes

1 cup each beef broth and dry red wine

Directions

1. Coat beef with flour.

2. Pour oil into pot. Set to STOVETOP HIGH and heat oil. Add beef to pot in batches. Cook uncovered 15 minutes or until browned on all sides. Remove beef from pot.

3. Add pancetta to pot. Cook uncovered until lightly browned, stirring occasionally. Stir in onion, carrots, garlic, oregano, red pepper, rosemary, and thyme and cook 3 minutes. Stir in tomato paste, tomatoes, broth, and wine.

4. Return beef to pot. Set to SLOW COOK LOW for 6 to 8 hours. Cover and cook until beef is fork-tender.

NINJA TIME-SAVER TIP

You can shorten the SLOW COOK step for this dish and cook on HIGH for 4 to 5 hours.

STOVETOP/OVEN

COD WITH ORANGE GLAZE & SNAP PEAS

Cod is a firm, white fish that stands up beautifully to the gingered orange glaze. The sauce reduces to a glaze in bottom of the pot while sugar snap peas steam on rack, creating an especially delicious dinner.

PREP: 10 minutes • **COOK:** 20 minutes • **SERVINGS:** 4

Ingredients

2 teaspoons canola oil

1 teaspoon ground ginger

2 cloves garlic, minced

1 bunch green onions, sliced

⅔ cup orange juice

⅓ cup water

2 teaspoons reduced-sodium soy sauce

1 tablespoon sugar

4 frozen uncooked cod fillets, 1-inch thick

2 cups sugar snap peas

Directions

1. Pour oil into pot. Set to STOVETOP HIGH and heat oil. Add ginger, garlic, and **half** the green onions to pot. Cook uncovered 3 minutes or until garlic is tender, stirring occasionally.

2. Stir orange juice, water, soy sauce, and sugar into pot. Place frozen fish into the multi-purpose pan. Place roasting rack into pot. Place pan on rack. Set OVEN to 325°F for 15 minutes. Cover and cook 5 minutes.

3. Place snap peas on top of fish. Cover and cook 5 minutes or until fish flakes easily when tested with fork and snap peas are tender-crisp, checking for doneness after 3 minutes of cooking time. Serve fish and snap peas with orange sauce and sprinkle with remaining green onions.

NINJA SERVING TIP

Frozen cod comes in different weights and thicknesses. For thicker fish, add an additional ½ cup water or orange juice to the glaze and add 2 to 4 minutes to the cooking time.

STEAM OVEN/STOVETOP

Entrees

GINGER, BOURBON, & BROWN SUGAR HOLIDAY HAM

Ham warms in the pot, its smoky flavor blending with the apple cider in the bottom of the pot. Fresh ginger, bourbon, and brown sugar are cooked down to make a beautiful glaze for the ham.

PREP: 10 minutes • **COOK:** 1 hour, 30 minutes • **SERVINGS:** 10

Ingredients

1 boneless, fully cooked ham (4 to 5 pounds)

2 cups cider, plus ½ cup

2 cups water, plus ½ cup

1 piece (3 inches) fresh ginger, peeled and finely grated

¼ cup bourbon

¼ cup packed brown sugar

Directions

1. Score ham on all sides in diamond pattern. Pour **2 cups** cider and **2 cups** water into pot. Place ham into pot. Set OVEN to 375°F for 1 hour, 30 minutes. Cover and cook until ham is hot. Remove ham from pot, cover, and keep warm. Discard remaining liquid in pot.

2. Stir ginger, bourbon, brown sugar, and remaining **1/2 cup** water and **1/2 cup** cider into pot. Set to STOVETOP HIGH. Cook uncovered 10 minutes or until mixture is reduced and thickened. Brush ham with brown sugar mixture.

NINJA SERVING TIP

Serve with baked sweet potatoes and green beans.

 SLOW COOK

CORNED BEEF & CABBAGE

Don't wait for holiday time to make this delicious one-pot meal!
It's so easy anytime you want something comforting — brisket,
potatoes, vegetables, and spices slow cook with no tending

PREP: 15 minutes • **COOK:** 4 hours, 40 minutes • **SERVINGS:** 6

Ingredients

2 celery stalks, cut into 3-inch pieces

1 cup baby carrots

1 onion, cut into wedges

6 small potatoes, cut in half

6 sprigs thyme or 1 teaspoon dried
   thyme leaves, crushed

1 corned beef brisket (about
   4 pounds) with pickling spice
   packet

½ head green cabbage, cut into
   wedges

Directions

1. Place celery, carrots, onion, potatoes, thyme, pickling spice into
   pot. Place beef into pot, fat side up. Add enough water to almost
   cover beef. Set to SLOW COOK HIGH for 4 to 5 hours. Cover
   and cook until beef is fork-tender.

2. Arrange cabbage over beef. Set to SLOW COOK HIGH for
   40 minutes. Cover and cook until cabbage is tender.

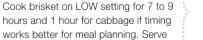 SERVING TIP

Cook brisket on LOW setting for 7 to 9
hours and 1 hour for cabbage if timing
works better for meal planning. Serve
with grainy mustard.

Entrees

CHICKEN ROULADE

This recipe features chicken with prosciutto rolled around a filling of spinach, roasted peppers, and sun-dried tomatoes and topped with a fresh tomato-basil sauce — all made quickly in the pot.

PREP: 40 minutes • **COOK:** 40 minutes • **SERVINGS:** 4

Ingredients

4 slices prosciutto

4 skinless, boneless chicken breast halves (about 6 ounces each), pounded thin

1 cup packed fresh baby spinach

1 cup roasted yellow peppers, cut into matchstick-thin strips

½ cup sun-dried tomatoes, cut into matchstick-thin strips

1 cup shredded Asiago cheese

Salt and ground black pepper

3 tablespoons olive oil

2 cups water

1 cup diced plum tomato

2 tablespoons thinly sliced basil leaves

Directions

1. Place prosciutto slices on work surface. Place **1** chicken breast half on **each** prosciutto slice. Layer **each** with spinach, peppers, sun-dried tomatoes, and cheese. Roll chicken and prosciutto around filling and secure with wooden picks. Season with salt and black pepper.

2. Pour **2 tablespoons** oil into pot. Set to STOVETOP HIGH and heat oil. Add chicken to pot, seam side up. Cook uncovered until browned. Remove chicken from pot.

3. Pour water into pot. Place chicken on roasting rack. Place rack into pot. Set OVEN to 350°F for 15 minutes. Cover and cook until chicken is cooked through and filling is hot. Turn off pot. Remove chicken from pot, cover, and keep warm.

4. Discard water from pot and wipe dry with paper towel, allowing it to cool before handling. Add remaining oil to pot. Set to STOVETOP HIGH. Add tomato to pot and season with salt and black pepper. Cook uncovered for about 6 minutes or until tomato mixture is warm. Stir in **1 tablespoon** basil. Slice chicken to serve. Top with tomato mixture and remaining basil.

NINJA TIME-SAVER TIP

Purchase the roasted peppers from the store olive bar and buy pre-shredded Asiago cheese.

HONEY ORANGE GLAZED CARROTS

CHAPTER 6:
Side Dishes

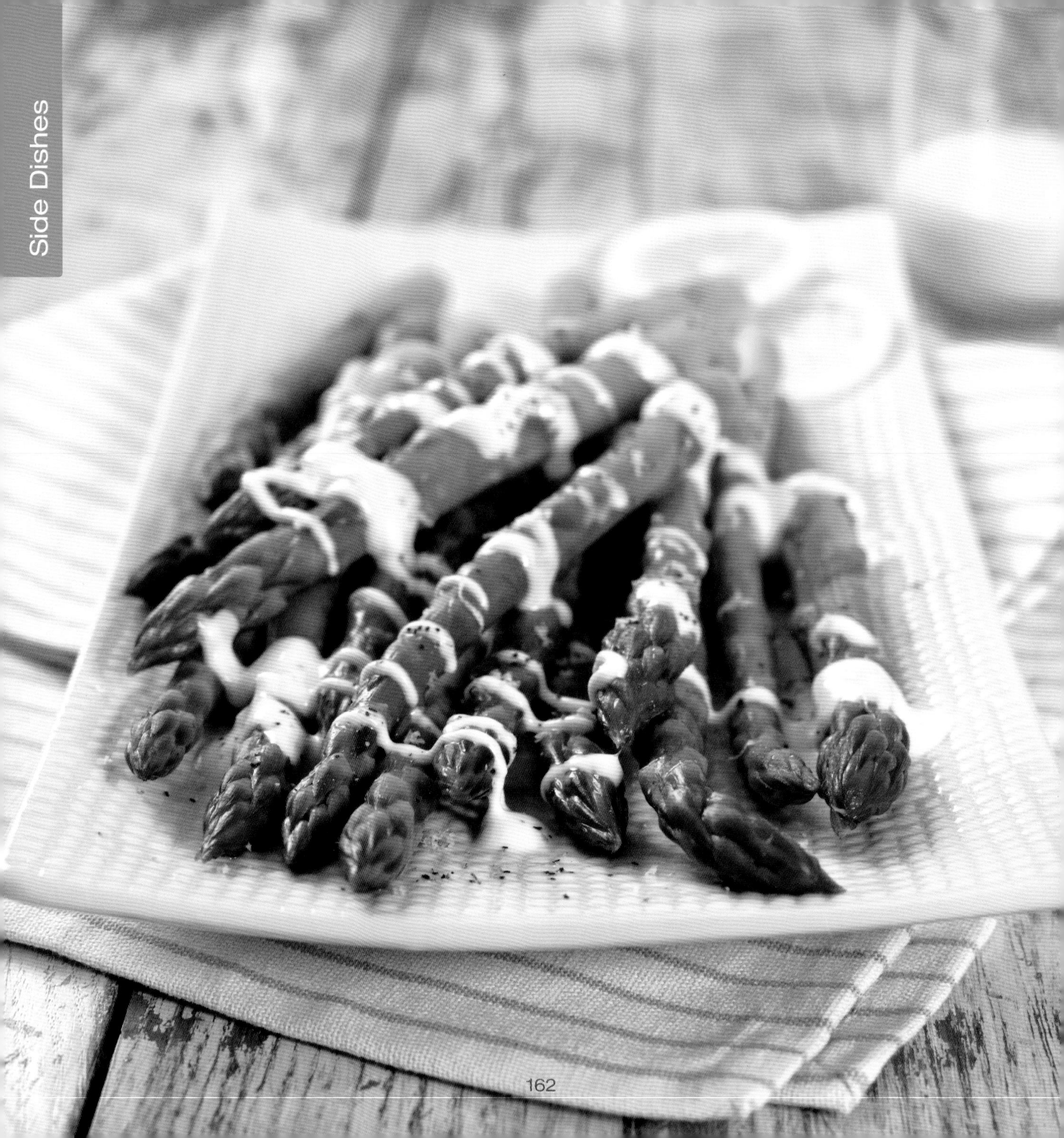

 STEAM OVEN

ASPARAGUS WITH LEMON AIOLI

Asparagus stays beautifully green and fresh — tasting even after cooking to tenderness — the secret is the steam! A lemony garlic sauce highlights its delicate flavor.

PREP: 10 minutes • **COOK:** 10 minutes • **SERVINGS:** 4

Ingredients

1 lemon

⅓ cup light mayonnaise

1 small garlic clove, minced

¼ teaspoon salt

Ground black pepper

1 cup water

1 pound asparagus, trimmed

Directions

1. Grate **½ teaspoon** zest and squeeze **2 teaspoons** juice from lemon into bowl. Stir in mayonnaise, garlic, and salt. Season with black pepper.

2. Pour water into pot. Place roasting rack into pot. Place asparagus on rack. Set OVEN to 350°F for 10 minutes. Cover and cook until asparagus is tender.

3. Season asparagus with additional salt and black pepper. Serve with lemon aioli.

NINJA TIME-SAVER TIP

Some stores carry pre-trimmed, washed fresh asparagus in the produce section. Try it to save on prep time!

 STOVETOP

BUTTERNUT SQUASH RISOTTO WITH BACON & SAGE

The butternut squash gives this risotto a lovely golden color. It cooks to creamy perfection in the pot with bacon and fresh sage.

PREP: 25 minutes • **COOK:** 1 hour, 5 minutes • **SERVINGS:** 6

Ingredients

- 1 tablespoon olive oil
- 2 medium onions, chopped
- 4 strips bacon, chopped
- 2 tablespoons chopped fresh sage leaves
- 1 cup uncooked Arborio rice
- ½ teaspoon salt
- ¼ teaspoon ground black pepper
- 4 cups chicken broth
- 2 cups peeled and chopped fresh butternut squash
- ¼ cup grated Parmesan cheese

Directions

1. Pour oil into pot. Set to STOVETOP HIGH and heat oil. Add onions, bacon, and sage to pot. Cook uncovered 10 minutes or until onions are tender, stirring occasionally. Stir rice, salt, and black pepper into pot. Cook uncovered 5 minutes, stirring often. Stir in broth. Cook 10 minutes.

2. Stir squash into pot. Set to STOVETOP LOW. Cover and cook 20 minutes or until rice and squash are tender.

3. Stir cheese into pot. Set to STOVETOP HIGH. Cook uncovered 10 minutes or until liquid is absorbed but mixture is creamy, stirring occasionally.

NINJA SERVING TIP

Serve sprinkled with additional chopped fresh sage leaves, if desired.

 STOVETOP

HONEY ORANGE GLAZED CARROTS

These carrots are so delicious, you will want to make them often — thank goodness they're so quick and easy! Carrot slices cook until tender in a glaze of orange, butter, honey, and thyme.

PREP: 10 minutes • **COOK:** 18 minutes • **SERVINGS:** 6

Ingredients

2 large oranges

1½ pounds carrots, peeled and cut into ½-inch thick slices

2 tablespoons butter

1 teaspoon salt

2 tablespoons honey

1 teaspoon fresh thyme leaves, minced, or ¼ teaspoon dried thyme

Directions

1. Grate ½ **teaspoon** zest and squeeze ¾ **cup** juice from oranges.

2. Stir carrots, **1 tablespoon** butter, orange juice, and salt in pot. Set to STOVETOP HIGH. Cover and cook 10 minutes or until carrots are tender-crisp, stirring occasionally.

3. Uncover pot. Cook uncovered until liquid is reduced to **2 tablespoons**. Stir in remaining butter, honey, orange zest, and thyme. Cook uncovered 3 minutes or until carrots are tender, stirring often.

NINJA SERVING TIP

These are wonderful served with rotisserie chicken breast and coleslaw purchased at the grocery store.

STOVETOP/OVEN

BRUSSELS SPROUTS WITH BACON & CARAMELIZED ONIONS

Bacon and caramelized onions cook first to lend their flavor to tender Brussels sprouts. It's an easy and inexpensive side dish that's special enough for company.

PREP: 10 minutes • **COOK:** 30 minutes • **SERVINGS:** 6

Ingredients

3 slices bacon, cut into ½-inch pieces

1 large onion, cut in half and thinly sliced

1 tablespoon olive oil

1½ pounds Brussels sprouts, trimmed and cut in half

¼ teaspoon salt

¼ teaspoon ground black pepper

Directions

1. Place bacon into pot. Set to STOVETOP HIGH. Cook uncovered 10 minutes or until crisp, stirring occasionally. Remove bacon from pot and drain on paper towels.

2. Add onion to pot. Cook uncovered 10 minutes or until deep brown and tender, stirring occasionally. Remove onion.

3. Add oil to pot. Stir in Brussels sprouts, salt, and black pepper. Set OVEN to 425°F for 10 minutes. Cover and cook until Brussels sprouts are tender-crisp, stirring once halfway through cooking time. Serve with onions and bacon.

NINJA SERVING TIP

For a flavor change, omit salt in recipe and stir in 1 tablespoon balsamic vinegar before serving.

STOVETOP/SLOW COOK

RATATOUILLE

Sautéing the vegetables in the pot first adds an extra layer of flavor to this French stewed vegetable dish. Eggplant, zucchini, peppers, and tomatoes simmer until meltingly tender with garlic, basil, and oregano.

PREP: 20 minutes • **COOK:** 4 hours, 15 minutes • **SERVINGS:** 10

Ingredients

2 tablespoons olive oil

1 medium onion, chopped

3 cloves garlic, sliced

1 eggplant (about 1½ pounds), cut into 1-inch pieces

2 medium zucchini, cut into 1-inch pieces

2 red peppers, cut into 1-inch pieces

1 teaspoon salt

1 can (28 ounces) can diced tomatoes, undrained

1 tablespoon tomato paste

½ teaspoon each ground black pepper and dried oregano leaves, crushed

¼ cup chopped fresh basil leaves

Directions

1. Pour oil into pot. Set to STOVETOP HIGH and heat oil. Add onion to pot. Cook uncovered 5 minutes or until onion is tender, stirring occasionally. Add garlic, eggplant, zucchini, peppers, and salt to pot. Cook 5 minutes or until vegetables are tender-crisp.

2. Stir tomatoes, tomato paste, black pepper, and oregano into pot. Set to SLOW COOK HIGH for 4 to 5 hours. Cover and cook until vegetables are tender. Stir in basil.

NINJA SERVING TIP

Serve ratatouille as a side dish or toss with pasta and cheese for a main dish.

Side Dishes

ITALIAN GREEN BEANS

Fresh green beans are quickly steamed to lock in flavor and nutrients, then tossed with a flavorful dressing and served warm or chilled.

PREP: 10 minutes • **COOK:** 15 minutes • **SERVINGS:** 4

Ingredients

1 cup water

1 pound fresh green beans, trimmed

1 tablespoon chopped fresh dill weed or 1 teaspoon dried dill weed

1 package (0.6 ounces) zesty Italian salad dressing mix, prepared according to package directions

Directions

1. Pour water into pot. Place roasting rack into pot. Place green beans on rack. Set OVEN to 350°F for 15 minutes. Cover and cook until the green beans are tender-crisp, checking for doneness after 10 minutes of cooking time.

1. Stir dill weed into dressing. Place green beans into bowl. Add **1/3 cup** dressing mixture and toss to coat. Reserve remaining dressing mixture for another use.

 SERVING TIP

The beans can be served at room temperature or chilled. Try adding toasted almonds for a nice crunch.

◎ 🔲 S T O V E T O P / O V E N

SEA SALT & CHILI ROASTED SWEET POTATO STRIPS

These crisp-on-the-outside, tender-on-the-inside sweet potato strips are sure to go fast at the table! The trick is to sear one side, then flip and bake. The seasonings add a spicy kick!

PREP: 10 minutes • **COOK:** 25 minutes • **SERVINGS:** 4

Ingredients

2 sweet potatoes (about 1¼ pounds), peeled and cut lengthwise into ½-inch slices, then into ½-inch strips

3 tablespoons olive oil

1½ teaspoons sea salt

½ teaspoon chili powder

Directions

1. Stir potatoes, olive oil, salt, and chili powder in bowl.

2. Place potato mixture into pot, arranging potatoes in single layer. Set to STOVETOP HIGH. Cook uncovered 10 minutes or until potatoes are lightly browned on bottom. Turn potatoes over. Set OVEN to 325°F for 15 minutes. Cover and cook until potatoes are browned and tender.

NINJA SERVING TIP

Serve with ketchup or sour cream for dipping.

 STOVETOP/OVEN

SCALLOPED POTATOES WITH MAPLE CREAM

The savory sweet cream sauce makes this a decadent dish. Potatoes and sweet potatoes provide a twist on traditional scalloped potatoes.

PREP: 10 minutes • **COOK:** 55 minutes • **SERVINGS:** 8

Ingredients

Cooking spray

4 large sweet potatoes (about 2 pounds), peeled and thinly sliced

4 large russet potatoes (about 2 pounds), peeled and thinly sliced

1½ cups heavy cream

½ cup pure maple syrup

1 tablespoon minced fresh rosemary leaves

1 teaspoon salt

¼ teaspoon ground black pepper

Directions

1. Spray the multi-purpose pan with cooking spray. Place **half** the sweet potatoes into pot. Top with **half** the russet potatoes. Repeat layers.

2. Stir cream, syrup, rosemary, salt, and black pepper in bowl. Pour cream mixture over potatoes. Set OVEN to 275°F for 50 minutes. Cover and cook until potatoes are tender. Set to STOVETOP HIGH. Cook 5 minutes or until potatoes are golden brown on bottom.

3. Invert potatoes onto serving platter.

 SERVING TIP

Serve a twist on this recipe at your Thanksgiving table! Substitute additional sweet potatoes for the russet potatoes. Top cooked sweet potato mixture with ½ cup toasted pecan pieces before serving.

STEAM OVEN/SLOW COOK

GARLICKY MASHED POTATOES

These creamy garlic mashed potatoes not only taste better than your old standby, but they are easier to make, too! The potatoes and garlic cook in the perfect amount of water, so there is no need to drain them before mashing.

PREP: 10 minutes • **COOK:** 30 minutes • **SERVINGS:** 12

Ingredients

5 pounds russet potatoes, peeled and diced

4 cloves garlic, peeled

2 cups water

½ cup butter, cut up

1½ cups hot milk or heavy cream

Salt and ground black pepper

Directions

1. Place potatoes, garlic, and water into pot. Set OVEN to 350°F for 30 minutes. Cover and cook until potatoes are tender. Turn off pot.

2. Mash potatoes with butter and milk. Season with salt and black pepper. Serve immediately or set to SLOW COOK BUFFET for 1 hour or until ready to serve.

NINJA HEALTHY TIP

Substitute chicken broth for milk or cream and reduce amount of butter to save some calories in a lighter version of this recipe. Yukon gold potatoes can also be substituted for the russets.

OVEN

EGGPLANT & ARTICHOKE PARMESAN

Enjoy flavors of Eggplant Parmesan without all the work — just assemble and bake! Eggplant and artichokes in a chunky tomato sauce are topped with bread crumbs and melted cheese — delicious!

PREP: 10 minutes • **COOK:** 50 minutes • **SERVINGS:** 6

Ingredients

1 large eggplant (about 1½ pounds), cut in ¾-inch pieces

1 jar (about 24 ounces) marinara sauce

1 can (14.5 ounces) diced tomatoes, undrained

1 can (about 14 ounces) artichoke hearts, rinsed, drained, and quartered

1 small onion, chopped

½ cup Italian-seasoned dry bread crumbs

1 cup shredded mozzarella cheese

½ cup grated Parmesan cheese

Directions

1. Place eggplant, sauce, tomatoes, artichokes, and onion in pot. Set OVEN to 325°F for 50 minutes. Cover and cook 40 minutes, stirring once halfway through cooking time.

2. Top with bread crumbs and cheeses. Cover and cook 10 minutes or until cheese is melted.

NINJA SERVING TIP

This tastes wonderful topped with ¼ cup toasted pine nuts.

 **STOVETOP/OVEN**

CUBAN BLACK BEANS & RICE

Sautéing the uncooked rice in the pot before adding water heightens the flavor of the finished dish. Mashing some of the beans before adding gives the dish a heartier texture.

PREP: 15 minutes • **COOK:** 40 minutes • **SERVINGS:** 6

Ingredients

1 tablespoon olive oil

1 large onion, chopped

1 large green or red pepper, chopped

4 cloves garlic, minced

1 cup uncooked regular long-grain white rice

1 teaspoon dried oregano, crushed

1 teaspoon ground cumin

¾ teaspoon salt

¼ teaspoon ground black pepper

2 cans (about 15 ounces each) black beans, rinsed and drained

2 cups water

1 can (about 15 ounces) diced tomatoes, undrained

Directions

1. Pour oil into pot. Set to STOVETOP HIGH and heat oil. Add onion and pepper to pot. Cook uncovered 10 minutes or until vegetables are tender-crisp, stirring occasionally. Add garlic to pot. Cook 2 minutes, stirring often. Stir in rice, oregano, cumin, salt, and black pepper. Cook 2 minutes, stirring often.

2. Place **1 cup** beans in bowl and coarsely mash with fork. Stir mashed beans, whole beans, water, and tomatoes in pot. Set OVEN to 350°F for 25 minutes. Cover and cook until liquid is absorbed and rice is tender, stirring occasionally after 15 minutes of cooking time.

 **NINJA** SERVING TIP

Serve sprinkled with chopped fresh cilantro leaves.

 **OVEN**

CRUSTY, CHEESY POTATOES AU GRATIN

Cream and Gruyère cheese are the stars in this decadent dish. Potatoes absorb the flavors as they cook to tenderness.

PREP: 15 minutes • **COOK:** 1 hour • **SERVINGS:** 4

Ingredients

1 cup shredded Gruyère or Cheddar cheese (about 4 ounces)

2 large russet potatoes or 4 Yukon Gold potatoes, peeled and thinly sliced

2 tablespoons butter, cut into small pieces

Salt and ground black pepper

¾ cup heavy cream

Directions

1. Spray 9x5 loaf pan with vegetable spray.

2. Layer cheese, potatoes, and butter in the pan as follows: **one-fourth** cheese, **one-third** potatoes, **half** butter. Repeat layers, seasoning with salt and black pepper. Top with remaining **¼ cup** cheese. Top with remaining potatoes. Pour cream over potatoes and sprinkle with remaining cheese. Cover pan with foil.

3. Place roasting rack into pot. Place pan on rack. Set OVEN to 375°F for 1 hour. Cover and cook until potatoes are tender.

NINJA SERVING TIP

Serve with grilled steaks and spinach and mushroom salad.

CARAMEL BAKED APPLES

CHAPTER 7: Desserts

STEAM OVEN/STOVETOP

Signature

BANANA LIME COCONUT BREAD

This tropical quick bread is finished with a decadent topping of butter, brown sugar, fresh lime, coconut, and pecans. Steam baking keeps the bread moist and tender, and the pecans in the topping add a nice crunch!

PREP: 10 minutes • **COOK:** 40 minutes • **SERVINGS:** 10

Ingredients

Cooking spray

Grated zest and juice of 2 limes

1 cup all-purpose flour

1½ teaspoons baking soda

Pinch salt

4 tablespoons butter

½ cup sugar

1 egg

½ ripe banana, mashed

⅔ cup skim milk

1 teaspoon vanilla extract

4 cups water

⅓ cup chopped toasted pecans

⅓ cup sweetened flaked coconut

¼ cup packed brown sugar

Directions

1. Spray multi-purpose pan with cooking spray. Stir flour, baking soda, and salt in a bowl.

2. Beat **2 tablespoons** butter and sugar in another bowl with electric mixer until mixture is creamy. Beat in egg.

3. Stir banana, milk, **half** the lime zest, **half** the lime juice, and vanilla extract in another bowl. Stir **half** the flour mixture and **half** the banana mixture into butter mixture. Repeat with remaining flour mixture and butter mixture. Pour batter into pan.

4. Pour water into pot. Place roasting rack into pot. Place pan on rack. Set OVEN to 375°F for 40 minutes. Cover and cook until wooden pick inserted in center comes out clean. Remove pan from pot. Let bread cool in pan on cooling rack 10 minutes.

5. Remove rack from pot and pour out water. Stir remaining butter, pecans, coconut, brown sugar, lime zest, and lime juice in pot. Set to STOVETOP HIGH. Cook uncovered 1 minute or until sugar is dissolved. Spoon coconut mixture over bread.

 **NINJA** SERVING TIP

This banana bread is great either as a breakfast or a dessert.

 **STEAM OVEN**

MAPLE PUMPKIN FLAN

These individual custards are perfect served as a special dessert for any autumn get-together. The water in the pot gently cooks the custard ensuring a creamy texture every time.

PREP: 10 minutes • **COOK:** 45 minutes **CHILL:** 4 hours • **SERVINGS:** 4

Ingredients

½ cup pure maple syrup

3 eggs

¾ cup canned pumpkin

½ cup milk

¼ cup sugar

1 teaspoon pumpkin pie spice

1 teaspoon vanilla extract

8 cups boiling water

Directions

1. Place **2 tablespoons** syrup in **each** of **4** (6-ounce) custard cups.

2. Beat eggs, pumpkin, milk, sugar, spice, and vanilla extract. Carefully pour pumpkin mixture into custard cups.

3. Pour water into pot. Place roasting rack into pot. Place custard cups on rack (water should cover about ¼ of the bottoms of the custard cups). Set OVEN to 350°F for 45 minutes. Cover and cook until custards are just set. Remove custard cups from pot. Let flans cool in cups on cooling rack 5 minutes.

4. Cover custard cups and refrigerate at least 4 hours or overnight. To serve, loosen edges of flans with a knife. Invert onto dessert plates.

NINJA SERVING TIP

Add some orange or lemon zest for a flavorful garnish.

 STEAM OVEN

MINI CHEESECAKES

This creamy cheesecake recipe is simple to put together, and the steam-baking technique ensures great results every time. Unlike traditional cheesecake recipes, the water bath stays in the bottom of the pot, so you don't have to deal with a pan full of hot water.

PREP: 15 minutes • **COOK:** 35 minutes **CHILL:** 4 hours • **SERVINGS:** 4

Ingredients

½ **cup graham cracker crumbs**

2 **tablespoons melted butter**

⅓ **cup sugar**

1½ **8-ounce packages cream cheese, softened**

1 **egg**

1 **teaspoon vanilla extract**

4 **cups water**

Directions

1. Cover outside of **2** (4-inch) springform pans with foil.

2. Stir graham cracker crumbs, butter, and **1 tablespoon** sugar in bowl. Press mixture into bottoms of pans.

3. Beat cream cheese with remaining sugar in bowl with electric mixer until smooth. Beat in egg and vanilla extract. Pour batter into pans.

4. Pour water into pot. Place roasting rack into pot and place filled pans on rack and cover. Set OVEN to 325°F for 35 minutes. **Do not lift lid during cooking.**

5. Remove pans from pot, let cool. Cover and refrigerate at least 4 hours or overnight.

NINJA SERVING TIP

Serve topped with fresh fruit (sliced strawberries, blueberries, or raspberries), fruit preserves, lemon curd, caramel sauce, toasted chopped pecans or mini chocolate chips.

 STEAM OVEN

DOUBLE-CHOCOLATE ZUCCHINI MUFFINS

These chocolaty muffins have a secret ingredient: shredded zucchini! Not only does it add good-for-you fiber, but the zucchini helps keep the muffins moist as they bake up light and tender in the pot.

PREP: 5 minutes • **COOK:** 25 minutes • **SERVINGS:** 6

Ingredients

- 1 package (6.5 ounces) chocolate chip muffin mix
- 2 tablespoons unsweetened cocoa powder
- ½ teaspoon ground cinnamon
- 1 medium zucchini, shredded
- ¼ cup water plus 2 cups water
- ½ teaspoon vanilla extract

Directions

1. Line 6-cup muffin pan with paper liners.

2. Stir muffin mix, cocoa powder and cinnamon in bowl. Stir in zucchini. Add ¼ **cup** water and vanilla extract and stir just until combined. Spoon batter into muffin pan cups, filling about 2/3 full.

3. Pour **2 cups** water into pot. Place roasting rack into pot. Place muffin pan on rack. Set OVEN to 375°F for 25 minutes. Cover and cook until wooden pick inserted in centers comes out clean. Immediately remove muffins from pan and let cool on cooling rack 10 minutes.

NINJA SERVING TIP

Serve with seedless raspberry jam for spreading.

STEAM OVEN

CHOCOLATE PEANUT BUTTER CUPCAKES

Two favorite flavors are reminiscent of childhood parties and the warmth of home-baked goodies! The pot's consistent heat distribution from the steam keeps the cupcakes cooking evenly.

PREP: 10 minutes • **COOK:** 20 minutes • **SERVINGS:** 6

Ingredients

½ cup all-purpose flour

½ cup sugar

2 tablespoons unsweetened cocoa powder

¼ teaspoon baking soda

¼ teaspoon salt

¼ cup milk

3 tablespoons creamy peanut butter

1 egg, beaten

1 teaspoon vanilla extract

2 cups water

1 cup prepared chocolate fudge frosting

Directions

1. Stir flour, sugar, cocoa powder, baking soda, and salt in bowl. Stir milk, **2 tablespoons** peanut butter, egg, and vanilla extract in another bowl. Stir milk mixture into flour mixture.

2. Line 6-cup muffin pan with paper liners. Spoon batter into liners.

3. Pour water into pot. Place roasting rack in pot and place pan onto rack. Set OVEN to 350°F for 20 minutes. Cover and cook until tops spring back when lightly touched. Remove pan from pot and let cool on cooling rack 15 minutes.

4. Stir frosting with remaining peanut butter in bowl.

NINJA SERVING TIP

Use peanut butter thinned with a little milk and sugar to frost cupcakes, then drizzle with melted chocolate.

SLOW COOK

APPLE CHERRY PASTRIES WITH PISTACHIOS

A warm compote of apples and dried cherries slow cooks with lemon and sugar before being spooned into pastry cups. A dollop of creamy vanilla pudding and sprinkle of chopped pistachios are the perfect finish!

PREP: 35 minutes • **COOK:** 2 hours • **SERVINGS:** 12

Ingredients

1 lemon

8 apples (about 3 pounds), peeled and cut into ¼-inch slices

½ cup dried cherries

1 cup sugar

1 package (3.4 ounces) vanilla instant pudding and pie filling mix

3 cups cold milk

2 packages (10 ounces each) frozen puff pastry shells, prepared according to package directions, cooled

½ cup shelled pistachio nuts, chopped

Directions

1. Grate ½ **teaspoon** zest from lemon.

2. Stir apples, cherries, sugar, and lemon zest in pot. Set to SLOW COOK HIGH for 2 to 3 hours. Cover and cook until apples are tender.

3. Beat pudding mix and milk in bowl 2 minutes or until mixture is thickened. Divide apple mixture among pastry shells. Top with pudding mixture and sprinkle with nuts.

NINJA SERVING TIP

Add different ingredients for a unique dessert; pear, dried cranberries, almonds... the possibilities are endless.

 STEAM OVEN

PECAN PIE BARS

Reminiscent of pecan pie, this quick-to-make dessert features brown sugar-glazed pecan filling and a biscuit-like crust — delicious!

PREP: 5 minutes • **COOK:** 45 minutes • **SERVINGS:** 10

Ingredients

¼ **cup butter, melted**

½ **cup packed brown sugar**

¼ **cup light corn syrup**

1 **cup pecan halves**

⅓ **cup all-purpose baking mix**

¾ **cup milk**

2 **eggs**

2 **cups water**

Directions

1. Stir butter, brown sugar, corn syrup, and pecan halves in bowl. Spread brown sugar mixture in bottom of multi-purpose pan.

2. Stir baking mix, milk, and eggs in bowl. Spread egg mixture over pecan mixture.

3. Pour water into pot. Place rack in pot and place multi-purpose pan on rack. Set OVEN to 400°F for 45 minutes. Cover and cook until center is set and springs back when lightly touched, and edges are lightly browned. Let cool 5 minutes, then invert onto a platter and cut into bars.

NINJA SERVING TIP
Serve with a dollop of whipped cream or low-fat whipped topping.

 STEAM OVEN

CAPPUCCINO MOLTEN LAVA CAKES

Take the guesswork out of baking molten chocolate cakes. The efficient heating in the pot bakes the outsides to perfection leaving a gooey chocolate-coffee center.

PREP: 5 minutes • **COOK:** 20 minutes • **SERVINGS:** 6

Ingredients

Cooking spray

1 cup semi sweet chocolate chips, melted

½ cup butter, melted

1 cup confectioners' sugar

2 eggs

2 egg yolks

2 tablespoons coffee-flavored liqueur

1 teaspoon vanilla extract

½ cup flour

2 cups water

Directions

1. Spray 6-cup muffin pan with cooking spray. Line bottoms of muffin pan cups with waxed paper circles and spray with cooking spray.

2. In a medium sized bowl, add chocolate and butter and stir until smooth. Stir in sugar. Stir in eggs and egg yolks. Stir in liqueur, vanilla extract, and flour. Spoon batter into muffin pan cups.

3. Pour water into pot. Place roasting rack into pot. Place pan on rack. Set OVEN to 425°F for 20 minutes. Cover and cook until sides of cakes are firm but centers are still soft. Remove pan from pot and let stand 2 minutes. Run knife around sides of cakes to loosen. Invert onto serving plate. Serve warm.

 SERVING TIP

Serve with whipped cream dusted with cinnamon. Try different flavors by substituting raspberry or hazelnut liqueur for the coffee-flavored liqueur.

STOVETOP

TROPICAL FRUIT & RICE PUDDING

Tropical fruit bits invigorate this traditional dessert.
The rice mixture is cooked until creamy in the steady
heat from the pot.

PREP: 10 minutes • **COOK:** 45 minutes • **SERVINGS:** 4

Ingredients

1 cup chopped packaged dried tropical fruit medley

1 cup uncooked Arborio or short-grain rice

3 cups water

¼ teaspoon salt

2 tablespoons butter, softened

1 can (14 ounces) sweetened condensed milk

1 teaspoon vanilla extract

Sweetened whipped cream or thawed frozen whipped topping

Sweetened flaked coconut, toasted

Directions

1. Place fruit into bowl and add hot water to cover. Let stand 5 minutes. Drain fruit well in colander.

2. Stir rice, water, and salt in pot. Set to STOVETOP HIGH. Cover and cook 30 minutes or until rice is tender and liquid is absorbed.

3. Stir butter, condensed milk, vanilla extract, and fruit into pot. Set to STOVETOP LOW. Cover and cook 10 minutes or until liquid is absorbed and mixture is creamy. Serve warm or at room temperature topped with whipped cream and coconut.

 SERVING TIP

Omit the whipped cream and coconut and sprinkle with ground cinnamon before serving.

STEAM OVEN

DULCE DE LECHE CAKE

This simplified version of the Latin American "Tres Leches" cake is drenched in cooked milk, steam baked to keep it moist, and served with plenty of fruit.

PREP: 10 minutes • **COOK:** 30 minutes **CHILL:** 4 hours • **SERVINGS:** 8

Ingredients

1 package (15.25 ounces) yellow butter cake mix

4 cups water

½ cup caramel sauce

½ cup heavy cream

2 cups mixed fresh berries (strawberries, raspberries, blueberries)

Whipped cream

Directions

1. Prepare cake mix batter according to package directions. Pour batter into multi-purpose pan.

2. Pour water into pot. Place roasting rack into pot and place multi-purpose pan on rack. Set OVEN to 350°F for 30 minutes. Cover and cook until toothpick inserted in center comes out clean; remove pan and rack from pot, empty water.

3. Add caramel sauce and heavy cream to pot. Set to STOVETOP MED. Stir constantly until sauce is warmed and fully incorporated. Keep sauce warm.

4. Poke holes all over cake using a straw or skewer, making sure to poke through to bottom of cake. Pour warm caramel mixture slowly all over cake so that it soaks into cake. Refrigerate cake 4 hours or overnight. Serve with berries and whipped cream.

NINJA HEALTHY TIP

You can follow reduced fat directions on cake mix package to prepare cake batter, if you prefer.

Desserts

SALTED CARAMEL DEVIL'S FOOD MINI CUPCAKES

Fleur de Sel is a special salt with an earthy, delicious flavor that perfectly complements the sweet caramel-cheese frosting.

PREP: 20 minutes • **COOK:** 11 minutes • **SERVINGS:** 36

Ingredients

1 cup flour

⅓ cup unsweetened cocoa

1 teaspoon baking soda

⅔ cup sugar

¼ cup butter, softened

½ cup egg substitute

1 teaspoon vanilla

½ cup skim milk

1¼ ounces semi-sweet chocolate, finely chopped

1½ cups water

⅓ (8 oz.) package fat-free cream cheese

⅓ (8 oz.) tub fat-free whipped topping

2 tablespoons plus 2 teaspoons caramel sauce, fat-free

2 tablespoons + 2 teaspoons sugar substitute

Directions

1. In a small bowl, sift together the flour, cocoa, baking soda, and salt.

2. Beat sugar and butter in a bowl at medium speed until combined. Add egg and vanilla, beating well. Add flour mixture and milk alternately to sugar butter mixture, until combined. Fold in chocolate.

3. Add batter into silicone petite muffin tray. Place the roasting rack in pot and set the pan on the rack. Add 1½ cups of water to the pot. Set OVEN to 350°F for 15 minutes, checking after 10 minutes. Cover and cook until a toothpick inserted in center comes out clean. Remove tray and let cool.

4. Beat cream cheese and caramel in a mixing bowl until soft. Add whipped topping and gently fold in, scraping down sided till combined. Top each cupcake with 2 tsp of frosting, drizzle of fat-free caramel sauce (optional), and a pinch of Fleur de Sel.

NINJA TIME-SAVER TIP

Melt the butter and the chocolate together to save a step.

Desserts

EASY CRÈME BRÛLÉE

Steam baking takes the place of a traditional water bath in this recipe, yielding velvety-smooth custards topped with caramelized sugar.

PREP: 5 minutes • **COOK:** 1 hour • **CHILL:** 2 hours • **SERVINGS:** 4

Ingredients

1¾ cups heavy cream

⅓ cup plus 4 teaspoons sugar

3 egg yolks

1 teaspoon vanilla extract

2 cups water

Directions

1. Pour heavy cream into microwavable bowl. Microwave on HIGH 3 minutes. Whisk in **1/3 cup** sugar until sugar is dissolved. Slowly whisk **1/3 cup** warm cream into egg yolks in another bowl. Whisk yolk mixture back into remaining cream mixture. Stir in vanilla extract. Pour cream mixture into **4** (6-ounce) ramekins.

2. Pour water into pot. Place roasting rack into pot and place ramekins on rack. Set OVEN to 325°F for 1 hour. Cover with lid and cook until just set. Remove ramekins from pot and let cool. Cover ramekins and refrigerate 2 hours.

3. Remove ramekins from refrigerator and let stand 20 minutes. Sprinkle remaining sugar over custards in ramekins. Use small cooking torch to caramelize the sugar, forming a candy shell.

NINJA SERVING TIP

If you don't have a torch, you can still serve these custards with a nice, caramelized sugar crust. Heat the broiler during stand time noted above. Sprinkle remaining sugar over custards in ramekins. Place ramekins onto baking sheet. Broil 2 minutes or until sugar is caramelized.

 OVEN

IMPOSSIBLE FRENCH APPLE PIE

Apples tossed with cinnamon-sugar bake under a biscuit-like crust, and are sprinkled with a walnut streusel. The pot cooks the apples until soft but keeps the crust tender and light.

PREP: 10 minutes • **COOK:** 55 minutes • **SERVINGS:** 8

Ingredients

2 large Granny Smith apples, peeled, cored, and thinly sliced

⅓ cup granulated sugar

1 teaspoon ground cinnamon

Cooking spray

1⅓ cups all-purpose baking mix

¾ cup milk

2 eggs, beaten

¼ cup butter, softened

¼ cup packed brown sugar

½ cup chopped walnuts

Directions

1. Stir apples, granulated sugar, and cinnamon in bowl. Spray multi-purpose pan with cooking spray. Place apple mixture into pan.

2. Stir **2/3 cup** baking mix, milk, and eggs in bowl. Pour batter over apple mixture.

3. Stir butter, brown sugar, remaining baking mix, and walnuts in bowl. Spoon walnut mixture over batter. Place roasting rack into pot and place multi-purpose pan onto rack. Set OVEN to 400°F for 55 minutes. Cover and cook until top springs back when lightly touched.

NINJA SERVING TIP

Top each serving with frozen vanilla yogurt.

STEAM OVEN

Signature

LIGHT KIWI LIME ANGEL FOOD CUPCAKES

These fun desserts are only 15 calories each! Because they cook so quickly, it is an easy and guilt-free pleasure to whip up for family and friends.

PREP: 10 minutes • **COOK:** 15 minutes • **SERVINGS:** 30

Ingredients

¼ cup cake flour (or all-purpose flour), sifted

3 tablespoons sugar

3 egg whites

¼ teaspoon vanilla extract

Pinch salt

¼ teaspoon cream of tartar

2 teaspoons lime zest

3 teaspoons lime juice

2 cups water

4 tablespoons powdered sugar

1 kiwi, peeled, thinly sliced, and cut into quarters (pie-shaped)

Directions

1. In a small bowl, combine cake flour with **1 tablespoon** sugar.

2. With an electric mixer set to high, beat egg whites, vanilla extract, salt, and cream of tartar until soft peaks form. Add **1 teaspoon** lime zest and **1 teaspoon** lime juice. Gradually add remaining 2 tablespoons sugar. Beat on high until mixture is fully incorporated, glossy, and stiff peaks are formed.

3. Fold in by hand flour and sugar mixture in thirds until fully incorporated, keeping batter as voluminous as possible.

4. Fill silicone mini-muffin tray with 1 tablespoon batter in each cup. Pour water into pot. Place roasting rack in pot and tray on rack. Set OVEN to 325°F for 15 minutes, checking after 12 minutes, and cook until cupcakes rise and a toothpick inserted in centers comes out clean. Remove mini cupcakes and let cool.

5. Stir together remaining lime zest, 2 teaspoons lime juice, and powdered sugar and frost the tops of the cakes. Top with kiwi.

NUTRITION PER SERVING: 15 CALORIES; 0G FAT; 0G SATURATED FAT; 10MG SODIUM; 4G CARBOHYDRATE; 0G FIBER; 0G PROTEIN

NINJA SERVING TIP

Cake flour will create a delicate, tender crumb, but all-purpose flour will work if that is what you have.

STEAM OVEN

KAHLÚA® BROWNIES WITH CINNAMON CREAM

A clever trick transforms box-mix brownies into an amazing dessert. Just replace water with coffee-flavored liqueur! Steam baking keeps brownies tender and moist.

PREP: 5 minutes • **COOK:** 2 hours • **SERVINGS:** 6

Ingredients

1 box (18 ounces) brownie mix

1 ounce Kahlúa® coffee liqueur

Cooking spray

1 cup water

¾ cup frozen whipped topping, thawed

½ teaspoon ground cinnamon

Directions

1. Prepare brownie batter according to package directions except replace half the water with liqueur. Spray nonstick 6-cup muffin pan with cooking spray. Pour batter into muffin pan, filling about 2/3 full.

2. Pour water into pot. Place roasting rack into pot and place pan on rack. Set OVEN to 350°F for 2 hours. Cover and cook until wooden pick inserted in centers comes out with moist crumbs. Remove pan from pot and let cool on cooling rack 10 minutes.

3. Stir whipped topping and cinnamon in small bowl. Cover and refrigerate until ready to serve. Serve brownies with cinnamon cream.

NINJA HEALTHY TIP

You can follow reduced-fat directions on the brownie mix package to prepare brownie batter, if you prefer.

 STEAM OVEN

OATMEAL BLUEBERRY BARS

Fresh blueberries bake with oats and brown sugar in this steam-baked recipe. Steam baking helps the bars to stay moist and full of blueberry flavor.

PREP: 10 minutes • **COOK:** 45 minutes • **SERVINGS:** 12

Ingredients

Cooking spray

¼ cup butter, melted

½ cup packed brown sugar

1 egg

1 teaspoon vanilla extract

¾ cup quick oats

½ cup all-purpose flour

⅛ teaspoon salt

1 package (6 ounces) fresh blueberries

2 cups water

Directions

1. Spray the multi-purpose pan with cooking spray.

2. Stir butter, brown sugar, egg, and vanilla extract in bowl. Stir in oats, flour, salt, and blueberries. Pour batter into pan.

3. Pour water into pot. Place roasting rack in pot and set pan onto rack. Set OVEN to 400°F for 45 minutes. Cover and cook until set in center and lightly browned at edges. Remove pan from pot and let cool on cooling rack for 15 minutes. Cut into bars to serve.

NINJA SERVING TIP

Serve topped with low-fat vanilla yogurt and additional blueberries.

OVEN

PEACH ALMOND COBBLER WITH COOKIE TOPPING

Frozen peaches make the prep easy in this recipe. The reserved juices thicken in the pot to make a delicious cobbler filling topped with crunchy cookie crumbs.

PREP: 10 minutes • **COOK:** 30 minutes • **SERVINGS:** 8

Ingredients

4 bags (16 ounces each) frozen sliced peaches, thawed and drained, juice reserved

2 tablespoons cornstarch

½ cup sugar

2 teaspoons almond extract

1 package (7 ounces) almond or sugar cookies, crushed (about 2 cups crushed)

Sweetened whipped cream

Directions

1. Stir reserved peach juice and cornstarch in pot. Add peaches, sugar, and almond extract and stir to coat. Set OVEN to 325°F for 30 minutes. Cover and bake until peaches are tender.

2. Turn off pot. Let peach mixture cool in pot 5 minutes. Sprinkle with cookie crumbs. Serve with whipped cream.

NINJA HEALTHY TIP

For a healthful twist, try using your favorite granola or chopped toasted almonds instead of almond cookies.

STEAM OVEN/STOVETOP

LIGHT CHOCOLATE LOAF WITH HAZELNUT PRALINE

This chocolate loaf cake is light and airy. For leftovers, wrap with plastic wrap, removing as much air as possible.

PREP: 15 minutes • **COOK:** 30 minutes • **SERVINGS:** 20

Ingredients

2 eggs

¾ cup sugar

1 cup flour

1 teaspoon baking powder

½ teaspoon salt

¼ cup bittersweet chocolate, melted

1 tablespoon butter, melted

½ cup skim milk

2¼ cups water

½ cup sugar

½ cup chopped toasted hazelnuts

Directions

1. In an electric mixer, beat the eggs with the sugar on medium speed until thick and pale yellow, about 10 minutes.

2. In a small bowl, sift together the flour, baking powder, and salt. In another small bowl, mix together melted chocolate and butter. Add the milk to the melted chocolate mixture and set aside.

3. Gradually add the flour mixture to egg and sugar mixture on low speed. Gently stir in chocolate mixture. Spray loaf pan with nonstick cooking spray and pour in batter. Add **2 cups** of water to the pot, place the roasting rack in the pot, and set the loaf pan on the rack. Set OVEN to 325°F for 25 minutes. Cover and cook until a toothpick stuck into the center of the cake comes out clean.

4. Clean pot. Set to STOVETOP MED and add sugar and **¼ cup water;** stir continuously until sugar melts and becomes a caramel. Add the hazelnuts and stir to coat. Spoon hot praline mixture over cake and let cool.

NINJA HEALTHY TIP

This loaf cake is very light in calories. Great for a breakfast, each slice is only about 100 calories.

 STOVETOP/OVEN

PEAR BLUEBERRY CRISP

The warm, sweet pear and blueberry mixture is sprinkled with a crunchy oatmeal-brown sugar topping. Both topping and filling are made right in the pot!

PREP: 20 minutes • **COOK:** 40 minutes • **SERVINGS:** 6

Ingredients

½ cup quick oats

½ cup plus 2 tablespoons packed dark brown sugar

¾ cup all-purpose flour

1 teaspoon ground nutmeg

1 teaspoon ground cinnamon

¼ cup plus 2 tablespoons butter, melted

3 pounds Bartlett pears, peeled, cored, and cut into ⅛-inch slices

1 package (6 ounces) fresh blueberries or 1 cup frozen blueberries

1 tablespoon lemon juice

Directions

1. Stir oats, **½ cup** brown sugar, flour, nutmeg, and cinnamon in pot. Stir in **¼ cup** butter. Set to STOVETOP HIGH. Cook uncovered 15 minutes or until oat mixture is golden, stirring occasionally. Remove oat mixture from pot and spread on plate. The oat mixture will still be soft, but will crisp and harden up as it cools.

2. Add remaining butter to pot. Set OVEN to 350°F for 20 minutes. Stir pears, blueberries, lemon juice, and remaining brown sugar in pot. Cover and cook 10 minutes.

3. Remove lid and cook uncovered 10 minutes or until liquid is reduced and pears are tender, stirring occasionally. Sprinkle pear mixture with oat mixture to serve.

NINJA SERVING TIP

You can make this recipe ahead and store cooked pear mixture covered in refrigerator until ready to serve. Oat mixture can be kept at room temperature in an airtight container.

 STEAM OVEN/STOVETOP

CARAMEL BAKED APPLES

Making caramel sauce sounds difficult — but not with this recipe. You can make the stuffed baked apples and the simple caramel sauce in the same pot — no extra saucepan to clean!

PREP: 15 minutes • **COOK:** 35 minutes • **SERVINGS:** 6

Ingredients

6 medium apples (about 3 pounds), cored

12 vanilla wafer cookies, finely crushed

¼ cup butter, melted

3 tablespoons raisins

½ teaspoon ground cinnamon

2 cups water

¼ cup packed dark brown sugar

18 caramels, unwrapped

Directions

1. Remove 1 strip of apple peel about 1 inch from top of each apple. Stir cookie crumbs, **2 tablespoons** butter, raisins, and cinnamon in bowl. Stuff **about 1 tablespoon** cookie crumb mixture into **each** apple.

2. Stir water, brown sugar, and remaining butter in pot. Place roasting rack into pot. Place stuffed apples on rack. Set OVEN to 350°F for 30 minutes. Cover and cook until apples are tender, checking for doneness after 10 minutes of cooking time.

3. Carefully remove apples and rack from pot. Add caramels to liquid in pot. Set to STOVETOP MED. Cook uncovered 5 minutes or until caramels are melted and mixture is smooth, stirring constantly with wooden spoon. Drizzle **2 tablespoons** caramel sauce over **each** apple.

NINJA SERVING TIP

Serve the apples and caramel sauce warm with vanilla ice cream or sweetened whipped cream.

 STEAM OVEN

GINGERBREAD WITH DRIED CHERRIES

The rich, spicy aroma will fill your kitchen when you bake this gingerbread in the pot until moist and flavorful. Dried cherries are a nice, tangy surprise.

PREP: 10 minutes • **COOK:** 30 minutes • **SERVINGS:** 8

Ingredients

Cooking spray

½ cup dried cherries

2 teaspoons all-purpose flour

1 package (14.5 ounces) gingerbread cake mix

3¼ cups water

1 egg

Directions

1. Spray the multi-purpose pan with cooking spray. Stir cherries and flour in bowl.

2. Stir cake mix, **1¼ cups** water, and egg in another bowl. Stir in cherry mixture. Pour batter into pan.

3. Pour remaining **2 cups** of water into pot. Place roasting rack into pot. Place pan on rack. Set OVEN to 350°F for 30 minutes. Cover and cook until a toothpick inserted in center comes out clean.

NINJA SERVING TIP

Serve with a dollop of whipped topping sprinkled with brown sugar.

MINI STRAWBERRY SHORTCAKES

Finding farm stands selling local in-season berries is worth the drive. Buy extra and freeze some for winter smoothies. This recipe is also short on calories with less than 50 each.

PREP: 10 minutes • **COOK:** 15 minutes • **SERVINGS:** 30

Ingredients

1 egg

⅓ cup sugar

½ cup flour

½ teaspoon baking powder

¼ cup skim milk

½ tablespoon butter, melted

½ teaspoon vanilla

2 cups water

½ cup heavy cream

1½ teaspoons sugar

15 strawberries, hulled and sliced ¼ inch

Directions

1. With an electric mixer, beat the egg with the sugar on medium speed until thick and pale yellow, about 5–10 minutes. In a small bowl, sift together the flour and baking powder.

2. In the meantime, stir together milk and butter; set aside.

3. Gradually add flour mixture to egg and sugar mixture on low speed. Gently stir in milk and butter mixture, then vanilla. Scoop **1 tablespoon** of batter each into silicone petite muffin tray.

4. Pour water into pot. Place rack in pot. Set muffin tray on rack. Set OVEN to 325°F for 15 minutes, cover and cook, checking after 10 minutes or until a toothpick stuck into the center of a cupcake comes out clean; let cool.

5. Beat heavy cream and **1½ teaspoons** of sugar together until peaks form. Top mini cupcakes with whipped cream and a slice of strawberry. Decorate as desired.

NINJA SERVING TIP

Swap out the strawberry with any fresh fruit that is ripe or in season as desired.

FRITTATA WITH HASH BROWNS & BACON

CHAPTER 8:
Breakfasts

 **STEAM OVEN**

BLUEBERRY PANCAKE MUFFINS

Buttermilk blueberry pancakes — in a muffin! These quick-to-make muffins bake up light and moist in the pot, thanks to the steam-baking technique.

PREP: 15 minutes • **COOK:** 25 minutes • **SERVINGS:** 6

Ingredients

1 cup all-purpose flour

1½ teaspoons baking powder

¼ teaspoon baking soda

¼ teaspoon salt

2 teaspoons sugar

¾ cup buttermilk

1 tablespoon canola oil

1 egg

3 tablespoons canned blueberries, drained

Cooking spray

1½ cups hot water

Directions

1. Stir flour, baking powder, baking soda, salt, and sugar in bowl.

2. Beat buttermilk, oil, and egg in another bowl. Add buttermilk mixture to flour mixture and stir just until combined. Stir in blueberries.

3. Spray 6-cup muffin pan with cooking spray. Spoon batter into muffin-pan cups.

4. Pour water into pot. Place roasting rack into pot. Place pan on rack. Set OVEN to 350°F for 25 minutes. Cover and cook until wooden pick inserted in centers comes out clean.

NINJA SERVING TIP

Sprinkle with confectioners' sugar and serve with maple butter.

 STOVETOP

 *Signature*

FRITTATA WITH HASH BROWN POTATOES & BACON

This Italian omelet is loaded with peppers, potatoes, bacon, and cheese. Cook everything in the pot — then stir in the eggs and cover to finish cooking — the frittata stays moist and delicious.

PREP: 15 minutes • **COOK:** 30 minutes • **SERVINGS:** 6

Ingredients

2 tablespoons canola oil

1 large onion, chopped

1 large green pepper, chopped

4 strips bacon, chopped

½ of a 32-ounce package frozen diced hash brown potatoes (about 3½ cups)

12 eggs

¾ cup milk

½ teaspoon salt

¼ teaspoon ground black pepper

1 cup shredded Cheddar cheese

Directions

1. Pour oil into pot. Set to STOVETOP HIGH and heat oil. Add onion, green pepper, and bacon to pot. Cook uncovered 15 minutes or until vegetables are tender, stirring often.

2. Stir in potatoes. Cover and cook 5 minutes.

3. Beat eggs, milk, salt, and black pepper in bowl. Set pot to STOVETOP MED. Stir egg mixture and cheese into pot. Cover and cook 10 minutes or until the egg mixture is set.

NINJA SERVING TIP

Serve topped with additional chopped cooked bacon, if desired.

 **STOVETOP/SLOW COOK**

BAKED BREAKFAST OATMEAL

Hearty steel-cut oats cook until tender in a mixture of hot milk, maple syrup, butter, vanilla, and spices. No need to stir; the mixture slow cooks perfectly. Sweet, tart dried cherries are the perfect finish.

PREP: 15 minutes • **COOK:** 2 hours, 10 minutes • **SERVINGS:** 4

Ingredients

4 cups milk

4 tablespoons pure maple syrup

2 tablespoons butter, cut up

2 teaspoons vanilla extract

1 teaspoon ground cinnamon

¼ teaspoon ground nutmeg

  Pinch salt

1 cup uncooked steel-cut oats

1 cup dried cherries

Directions

1. Stir milk, syrup, butter, vanilla extract, cinnamon, nutmeg, and salt in pot. Set to STOVETOP HIGH. Cover and cook 10 minutes or until butter is melted.

2. Stir in oats. Set to SLOW COOK HIGH for 2 to 3 hours. Cover and cook until oats are tender and mixture is creamy. Stir in cherries.

 NINJA SERVING TIP

Try adding cut-up bananas, apples, pears, or raisins. For creamier oatmeal, stir in a touch of milk with each serving.

218

 STEAM OVEN

DATE NUT LOAF

This quick, moist breakfast cake is packed with dates and pecans.
Place the pan with the batter right in the pot, cover, and bake.

PREP: 20 minutes • **COOK:** 35 minutes • **SERVINGS:** 12

Ingredients

Cooking spray

2 cups plus 1 tablespoon all-
   purpose flour

1 cup chopped dried pitted dates

½ cup orange juice

½ teaspoon vanilla extract

1 teaspoon baking powder

1 teaspoon ground cinnamon

½ teaspoon baking soda

½ teaspoon salt

⅔ cup chopped pecans

2 tablespoons butter, softened

⅔ cup packed brown sugar

1 large egg

Directions

1. Spray 9x5 loaf pan with cooking spray and coat with **1 tablespoon** flour. Stir dates, orange juice, and vanilla extract in bowl.

2. Stir **2 cups** flour, baking powder, cinnamon, baking soda, and salt in bowl and add pecans.

3. Beat butter, brown sugar, and egg in bowl with electric mixer until creamy. Stir in date mixture. Gradually add flour mixture, stirring well after each addition. Spoon batter into loaf pan.

4. Pour 2 cups water into pot. Place rack into pot and place loaf pan on rack. Set OVEN to 350°F, and bake for 35 minutes. Cover and cook or until a toothpick inserted in center comes out clean.

5. Remove pan from pot and let cool on rack for 5 minutes. Remove loaf from pan and let cool completely.

NINJA SERVING TIP

For Cream Cheese Icing: Beat ½ of an 8-ounce package of softened cream cheese, ¼ cup softened butter, and ½ teaspoon vanilla extract in a bowl with electric mixer until creamy, Gradually and 2½ cups of confectioners' sugar and beat until smooth.

 **STOVETOP / STEAM OVEN**

CREAMY BAKED EGGS

Baked eggs are made more sumptuous with a dollop of cream and a sprinkle of crisp bacon. Steam baking helps the eggs cook more evenly.

PREP: 10 minutes • **COOK:** 20 minutes • **SERVINGS:** 4

Ingredients

2 strips bacon

4 tablespoons heavy cream or half and half

4 eggs

Salt and ground black pepper

Ground nutmeg

1 cup water

Directions

1. Place bacon strips into pot. Set to STOVETOP HIGH. Cook uncovered 10 minutes or until bacon is crisp on both sides. Remove bacon from pot and drain on paper towels. Crumble bacon.

2. Spoon **1 tablespoon** cream into **each** of **4** custard cups. Crack **1** egg into **each** cup. Season with salt, black pepper, and nutmeg.

3. Pour water into pot. Place roasting rack into pot. Place custard cups on rack. Set OVEN to 400°F for 10 minutes. Cover and cook until eggs are set, checking after 5 minutes for softly set. Sprinkle with bacon.

NINJA SERVING TIP

Sprinkle baked eggs with finely shredded Swiss cheese and chopped fresh basil.

STOVETOP/SLOW COOK

APPLE FRENCH TOAST CASSEROLE

This warm bread pudding is perfect for a special breakfast or brunch. Apples and pecans cook in the pot with a maple-butter sauce, then are tossed with cubes of challah in a spiced milk mixture. Cover and let the sweet aroma fill your kitchen as it cooks.

PREP: 20 minutes • **COOK:** 2 hours, 10 minutes • **SERVINGS:** 6

Ingredients

½ cup butter

2 Granny Smith apples, peeled, cored, and chopped

1 cup chopped pecans

½ cup packed brown sugar

½ cup pure maple syrup

1 loaf challah bread (about 1 pound), cut into cubes

6 large eggs

2 cups milk

2 teaspoons ground cinnamon

1 tablespoon vanilla extract

Pinch salt

Confectioners' sugar

Directions

1. Place butter into pot. Set to STOVETOP HIGH and heat until butter is melted. Place apples, pecans, brown sugar, and syrup in pot. Cook uncovered 10 minutes or until apples are tender, stirring often.

2. Place bread in bowl. Beat eggs, milk, cinnamon, vanilla extract, and salt in another bowl. Pour egg mixture over bread and stir to coat. Pour bread mixture into pot and stir. Set to SLOW COOK HIGH for 2 to 3 hours. Cover and cook until center is set. Turn off pot. Let stand 10 minutes before serving. Sprinkle with confectioners' sugar.

NINJA HEALTHY TIP

Use refrigerated egg substitute in place of eggs and 1% milk instead of whole as a healthier swap of ingredients.

STOVETOP

BROCCOLI CHEESE SCRAMBLED EGGS

Simply cook the broccoli in the pot, add the eggs and tangy shredded Cheddar, and breakfast is ready — in 15 minutes!

PREP: 5 minutes • **COOK:** 10 minutes • **SERVINGS:** 4

Ingredients

1 package (12 ounces) frozen broccoli florets

2 tablespoons butter

Salt and ground black pepper

8 eggs

2 tablespoons milk

¾ cup shredded white Cheddar cheese

Crushed red pepper (optional)

Directions

1. Place broccoli and butter into pot and season with salt and black pepper. Set to STOVETOP MED. Cover and cook 10 minutes or until broccoli is tender, stirring occasionally.

2. Beat eggs and milk in bowl. Stir egg mixture in pot. Cook uncovered 2 minutes or until egg mixture is set, stirring often. Stir in cheese. Season with salt, black pepper, and red pepper, if desired.

NINJA HEALTHY TIP

Substitute egg whites for half the eggs and omit cheese.

 STOVETOP/OVEN

CARAMELIZED ONION FRITTATA

The steady heat in the pot allows the sugars in the onions to caramelize without scorching, resulting in deeply browned onions with spectacular flavor. Stir in the eggs and Gruyère cheese and bake to make a perfect Italian omelet!

PREP: 10 minutes • **COOK:** 30 minutes • **SERVINGS:** 8

Ingredients

12 eggs

Salt and ground black pepper

2 tablespoons butter

1 tablespoon canola oil

4 onions, thinly sliced

1 tablespoon chopped fresh thyme leaves

1½ cups grated Gruyère cheese

Chopped fresh chives

Directions

1. Beat eggs in bowl. Season with salt and black pepper.

2. Place butter and oil into pot. Set to STOVETOP HIGH and heat until butter is melted. Add onions and thyme to pot and season with salt and black pepper. Cook uncovered 20 minutes or until onions are deep brown and tender, stirring occasionally.

3. Stir eggs in pot. Cook 1 minute. Stir in cheese. Set OVEN to 325°F for 10 minutes, checking after 7 minutes. Cover and cook until egg mixture is set, stirring once halfway through cooking time.

4. Invert frittata onto serving platter. Sprinkle with chives.

 SERVING TIP

Butter a slice of toasted Italian bread and place a frittata square in the middle for the perfect Italian egg sandwich.

 STEAM OVEN

LOW-FAT SPICED MAPLE CORN MUFFINS

Start with a box of packaged corn muffin mix, then spice it up with maple syrup and cinnamon for a new favorite breakfast treat. The pot insulates as it bakes, which means that your corn muffins are always moist.

PREP: 5 minutes • **COOK:** 15 minutes • **SERVINGS:** 6

Ingredients

Cooking spray

1 package (6.5 ounces) cornbread and muffin mix

2 egg whites

¼ cup fat-free milk

¼ cup pure maple syrup

1 teaspoon ground cinnamon

2 cups water

Directions

1. Spray 6-cup muffin pan with cooking spray.

2. Stir muffin mix, egg whites, milk, syrup, and cinnamon in bowl. Spoon batter into muffin-pan cups.

3. Pour water into pot. Place roasting rack into pot. Place pan onto rack. Set OVEN to 400°F for 15 minutes. Cover and bake until wooden pick inserted in centers comes out clean.

NINJA SERVING TIP

Serve with your favorite fruit butter, like apple butter or pumpkin butter.

224

STOVETOP

CORNED BEEF HASH BREAKFAST

This updated version of corned beef hash features chopped corned beef stirred into eggs scrambled with sour cream. The potatoes are hash brown patties that are cooked from frozen right in the pot, then served as a side dish. Breakfast is served!

PREP: 10 minutes • **COOK:** 20 minutes • **SERVINGS:** 4

Ingredients

2 tablespoons butter

4 frozen hash brown potato patties

¼ pound sliced corned beef, chopped

4 eggs

½ cup sour cream

¼ cup chopped green onions

Salt and ground black pepper

Directions

1. Place butter into pot. Set to STOVETOP HIGH and heat until butter is melted. Add potato patties to pot. Cook uncovered 10 minutes or until crisp on both sides. Remove potato patties from pot and keep warm.

2. Place corned beef into pot. Cook for 1 minute or until hot.

3. Stir eggs, sour cream, green onions, salt, and black pepper in bowl. Stir egg mixture into pot. Cover and cook 4 minutes or until eggs are set. Serve patties with egg mixture.

 **NINJA** SERVING TIP

Serve with sliced fresh tomatoes or fresh mixed fruit.

STEAM OVEN

SWEET POTATO BISCUITS

The beautiful orange color of these biscuits makes them perfect for a holiday table. Steam baking keeps them meltingly moist and tender.

PREP: 10 minutes • **COOK:** 20 minutes • **SERVINGS:** 8

Ingredients

1 cup all-purpose flour

1 tablespoon sugar

1 teaspoon baking powder

¼ teaspoon salt

⅓ cup mashed cooked sweet potatoes

2 tablespoons butter, melted

⅓ cup milk

Cooking spray

1 cup water

Directions

1. Stir flour, sugar, baking powder, and salt in bowl. Stir sweet potatoes, butter, and milk in another bowl. Add sweet potato mixture to flour mixture and stir until just combined.

2. Spray the multi-purpose pan with cooking spray. Drop sweet potato mixture in pan to make 8 biscuits.

3. Pour water into pot. Place roasting rack into pot and set multi-purpose pan on rack. Set OVEN to 400°F for 20 minutes. Cover and cook until biscuits are cooked through.

NINJA SERVING TIP

Serve with Orange Honey Butter: Stir ¼ cup softened butter, 2 teaspoons honey, and ½ teaspoon grated orange zest in bowl.

 **STEAM OVEN**

WHOLE WHEAT GRANOLA & CHERRY MUFFINS

Whole wheat flour and granola add texture to these homemade muffins, but baking in the pot keeps them light and moist. Fresh cherries convey the sweet taste of summer.

PREP: 10 minutes • **COOK:** 25 minutes • **SERVINGS:** 6

Ingredients

Cooking spray

1 cup whole wheat flour

½ cup all-purpose flour

¼ cup packed brown sugar

1 teaspoon baking powder

¼ teaspoon baking soda

¼ teaspoon salt

1 egg

1 cup milk

2 tablespoons vegetable oil

1 teaspoon vanilla extract

½ cup plus 2 tablespoons granola

2 cups water

1 cup fresh cherries, pitted and cut in half

Directions

1. Spray 6-cup muffin pan with cooking spray. Stir whole wheat flour, all-purpose flour, brown sugar, baking powder, baking soda, and salt in bowl.

2. Beat egg, milk, oil, and vanilla extract in another bowl. Add egg mixture to flour mixture and stir just until combined. Stir in **½ cup** granola and cherries. Spoon batter into muffin-pan cups. Sprinkle with remaining granola.

3. Place water in pot. Place roasting rack in pot and cupcakes on rack. Set OVEN to 400°F for 25 minutes. Cover and cook until a toothpick inserted into centers comes out clean. Remove, let cool on rack, and garnish with remaining **2 tablespoons** of granola.

NINJA TIME-SAVER TIP

Substitute thawed frozen or dried cherries for the fresh cherries.

 OVEN

MAPLE CINNAMON SCONES

Baking scones in the pot keeps them light and tender.
Enjoy the flavors of maple, cinnamon, and pecans for a
good start to your day.

PREP: 10 minutes • **COOK:** 15 minutes • **SERVINGS:** 6

Ingredients

1 cup flour

2 tablespoons sugar

1 teaspoon baking powder

1 teaspoon ground cinnamon

¼ teaspoon salt

¼ cup butter, cut into small pieces

¼ cup heavy cream or milk

2 tablespoons pure maple syrup

1 egg, beaten

½ cup chopped pecans

Directions

1. Place flour, sugar, baking powder, cinnamon, and salt in bowl.
Cut in butter with pastry blender or 2 knives until mixture
resembles coarse crumbs. Stir cream, syrup, and egg in another
bowl. Add pecans and cream mixture to flour mixture and stir just
until combined.

2. Drop dough by tablespoons into pot to make 6 scones. Set
OVEN to 300°F for 15 minutes. Cover and cook until scones are
golden brown. Remove scones from pot and let cool on cooling
rack for 5 minutes.

NINJA SERVING TIP

Serve scones with maple butter:
Soften 3 tablespoons butter and stir
in 1 teaspoon pure maple syrup.

TURKEY SAUSAGE, EGG, & CHEESE STRATA

This one-pot breakfast features eggs, sausage, tomatoes, cheese, and bread for a hearty start to your day and is especially great for weekend brunch.

PREP: 20 minutes • **COOK:** 2 hours, 20 minutes • **SERVINGS:** 6

Ingredients

1 tablespoon canola oil

1¼ pounds turkey sausage, casing removed

1 medium onion, chopped

1 tablespoon chopped garlic

2 medium plum tomatoes, chopped

1 tablespoon dried basil leaves, crushed

10 eggs, beaten

2 cups milk

5 cups sliced Italian bread cut into ½-inch pieces

1 cup shredded Monterey Jack cheese

Salt and ground black pepper

Directions

1. Pour oil into pot. Set to STOVETOP HIGH and heat oil. Add sausage to pot. Cook uncovered 10 minutes or until sausage is cooked through, stirring occasionally. Remove sausage from pot.

2. Stir onion, garlic, tomatoes, and basil in pot. Cook uncovered 5 minutes or until onion is tender, stirring occasionally. Remove vegetable mixture from pot.

3. Stir eggs, milk, bread, cheese, salt, and black pepper in bowl. Stir in sausage and vegetable mixture. Pour egg mixture into pot. Set to SLOW COOK HIGH for 2 to 3 hours. Cover and cook until mixture is set.

NINJA SERVING TIP

For a spicy dish, use hot Italian sausage instead of turkey sausage.

 STEAM OVEN

SOUR CREAM COFFEE CAKE

This coffee cake features a clever twist on streusel topping — crumbled cinnamon graham crackers! The sour cream cake bakes up with a velvety texture, thanks to steam baking, and crumbled graham crackers add a nice cinnamon crunch!

PREP: 10 minutes • **COOK:** 45 minutes • **SERVINGS:** 8

Ingredients

1¼ cups flour

½ teaspoon baking powder

½ teaspoon baking soda

¼ teaspoon salt

¼ cup butter, softened

½ cup packed brown sugar

1 egg

1 cup sour cream

½ cup milk

1 teaspoon vanilla extract

Cooking spray

3 cinnamon graham crackers, crushed

2 cups water

Directions

1. Stir flour, baking powder, baking soda, and salt in bowl.

2. Beat butter, brown sugar, and egg in bowl with electric mixer until mixture is creamy. Stir in sour cream, milk, and vanilla extract. Stir in flour mixture.

3. Spray the multi-purpose pan with cooking spray. Pour batter into pan. Sprinkle with graham cracker crumbs.

4. Pour water into pot. Place roasting rack into pot and set multi-purpose pan on rack. Set OVEN to 400°F for 45 minutes. Cover and cook until center is set and edges are lightly browned.

NINJA TIME-SAVER TIP

Purchase already-crushed graham cracker crumbs for topping. Use ½ cup crumbs and stir in ¼ teaspoon ground cinnamon, if desired.

 **SLOW COOK**

CHOCOLATE CHUNK & RASPBERRY STRATA

Layer bread slices with raspberry jam and chocolate, then soak in spiced milk mixture — all assembled in our pot, which acts as baking dish and oven in one!

PREP: 15 minutes • **COOK:** 1 hour • **SERVINGS:** 6

Ingredients

Butter

4 eggs

1½ cups milk

2 teaspoons ground cinnamon

1 tablespoon vanilla extract

Pinch salt

¼ cup maple-flavored syrup

1 loaf (16 ounces) good-quality sliced white bread

1 tablespoon butter

½ cup semi sweet chocolate chunks

½ cup seedless red raspberry jam

Directions

1. Butter bottom and sides of pot.

2. Beat eggs, milk, cinnamon, vanilla extract, salt, and syrup in bowl. Place half the bread slices into pot. Sprinkle with chocolate. Spoon jam over bread. Top with remaining bread slices. Pour egg mixture over bread slices.

3. Set pot to SLOW COOK HIGH for 1 to 2 hours. Cover and cook until mixture is set.

NINJA HEALTHY TIP

Use refrigerated egg substitute instead of eggs and 1% or fat-free milk instead of whole milk.

CHAPTER 9:
Charts & Index

Steam Infused Roasting

Cooking Infusions

Protein	Flavor Choice	Liquid	Seasoning	Extra Flavor Ingredients
CHICKEN *1 hour cooktime for 3-4 lbs.* *Steam Oven at 375°F*	Tuscan	3 cups White Wine, ½ cup Lemon Juice	1 cup Arugula	1 cup Fennel, 1 cup Pear
	Mediterranean	4 cups Chicken Broth	2 tsp. dried Oregano	½ cup Feta Cheese
	Caribbean	2 cups Orange Juice, 2 cups Broth	1 cup Onion, 2 cups Bell Pepper	2 Tb. Cumin, 1 cup Cilantro
	Thai	2 cans Coconut Milk, ½ cup Water	1½ Tb. minced Ginger	¼ cup Curry Paste
FISH *30 minutes cooktime for 2 lbs.* *Steam Oven at 350°F*	Southern	2 cups Fish Stock	½ cup Onion	½ cup Bacon, 1 cup Corn
	French	2 cups White Wine	1 cup Leek	1 cup Mushrooms
	Italian	2 cups Broth	2 tsp. dried Basil, 2 minced Garlic Cloves	1 can Cannellini Beans undrained, ½ pkg. frozen Spinach
	Lemon Dill	1½ cups Wine, ½ cup Lemon Juice	1 Tb. chopped Dill	1 Tb. Dijon Mustard
PORK *40 minutes cooktime for 2-3 lbs.* *Steam Oven at 375°F*	German	4 cups Chicken Broth	2 minced cloves Garlic, 1 tsp. Allspice	2 cups Onion
	Sweet/Savory	4 cups Apple Juice	1 cup Onion	4 cups Red Cabbage
	American	2 cups Broth, 2 cups Barbeque Sauce	2 minced Garlic Cloves	½ cup Bacon
	French	4 cups Chicken Broth	4 Cloves	¼ cup Honey Mustard
BEEF *40 minutes cooktime for 2-3 lbs.* *Steam Oven at 350°F*	Mexican	2 cups Salsa, 2 cups Beef Broth	2 Tb. chopped Chilies, 2 tsp. Cumin	2 minced Garlic Cloves, ½ cup Cilantro
	Asian	2 cups Teriyaki Sauce, 2 cups Water	½ cup Green Onions, 4 minced Garlic Cloves	½ Tb. minced Ginger, 2 Tb. Hot Garlic Paste
	Greek	3 cups Red Wine, 1 cup Water	1 can Tomato Paste, 2 Tb. Olive Oil	2 Tb. chopped Rosemary
	Spain	1 can diced Tomatoes, 2 cups Chicken Broth	2 cups Red Bell Pepper, 4 minced Garlic Cloves	1 cup Sherry, 2 tsp. Saffron

Steam Roast Flavor Substitutes

Have fun with the recipes and take something from ordinary to extraordinary with the quick change of a rub, sauce, flavorful infusion, crispy crust, or warm topping. Try out some of the recommendations below to change up one of your favorites or create a new one!

Flavor Substitutes

Rubs	Sauces & Glazes	Crispy Crust	Hot Warm Crust
Whether you are Sear/Cooking, Steam or Oven Roasting, these rubs will definitely kick your meal up a notch.	Baste your meat or fish with these sauces for an extra kick 15–30 minutes before they are done cooking when using your Roast mode.	Precrisp in the STOVETOP HIGH setting till golden brown, then just sprinkle over cooked meats, fish, or vegetables	Place on meat or vegetables 5 minutes before cooking is done.
Lemon Pepper Seasoning	Barbeque Sauce	Ritz, Butter, Parsley	Blue Cheese, Honey
Cajun Seasoning	Southwest Barbeque (blended with Chipotle in Adobo Purée, cumin, and lime juice)	Panko, Butter, Italian Seasoning, Parmesan	Gorgonzola, Walnut
Montreal Seasoning		Panko, Hazelnut, Butter,	Fontina, Garlic,
Peppercorn		Salt, Pepper	Sautéed Spinach
Asian Five Spice Seasoning & Orange Peel	Korean Barbeque	Sesame (Black and White)	Country Dijon Herb
Garlic, Parsley, Parmesan	Hoisin	Almond, Parsley, Lemon Peel	Pesto
Dijon Herb (Try Parsley, Herb de Provence, or Rosemary)	Sweet Chili Sauce	Za'tar, Pistachio	
		Coconut, Macadamia Nut	
		Panko, Coconut, Cayenne	

Charts

Slow Cooker Cooking Guide

Beef		
Type of Beef	Cook Time LOW	Cook Time HIGH
Top Round	8–10 hours	4–5 hours
Bottom Round	8–10 hours	4–5 hours
Chuck	8–10 hours	4–5 hours
Stew Meat (Beef, Lamb, Veal, Rabbit)	7–9 hours	3–4 hours
Eye of the Round, Sirloin	6–8 hours	3–4 hours
Short Ribs	7–9 hours	3½–4½ hours
Brisket	7–9 hours	3½–4½ hours
Pot Roast	7–9 hours	3½–4½ hours
Frozen Meatballs (precooked)	6–8 hours	3–4 hours

Pork		
Type of Pork	Cook Time LOW	Cook Time HIGH
Baby Back Ribs	7–9 hours	3½–4½ hours
Country Ribs	7–9 hours	3½–4½ hours
Pork Tenderloin	6–7 hours	3–4 hours
Pork Loin	7–9 hours	3½–4½ hours
Pork Rib Roast	7–9 hours	3½–4½ hours
Pork Butt	10–12 hours	5–6 hours
Pork Shoulder	10–12 hours	5–6 hours
Ham (fully cooked)	5–7 hours	2½–3½ hours
Ham, Bone-In (uncooked)	7–9 hours	3½–4½ hours

Slow Cooker Cooking Guide

Poultry

Type of Poultry	Cook Time LOW	Cook Time HIGH
Boneless, Skinless Breast	6–7 hours	3–4 hours
Boneless, Skinless Thighs	6–7½ hours	3–4½ hours
Bone-In Breast	6–7½ hours	3–4½ hours
Bone-In Thighs	7–9 hours	3½–4½ hours
Whole Chicken	7–9 hours	3½–4½ hours
Chicken Wings	6–7 hours	3–4 hours
Turkey Breast	7–9 hours	3½–4½ hours
Turkey Thighs	7–9 hours	3½–4½ hours

Fish

Type of Fish	Cook Time LOW	Cook Time HIGH
1-inch Fillets	---	30–45 minutes
Frozen Shrimp	Add during last 20–30 minutes of cooking	Add during last 20–30 minutes of cooking
Fresh Shellfish	Add during last 20–30 minutes of cooking	Add during last 20–30 minutes of cooking

Layered Meals

Prepare complete meals in a single pot on the OVEN setting by choosing a protein, a vegetable, and a starch from the chart below and layering them in the pot to cook together at the same time. Thicker protein and vegetables will require slightly longer cook times; adjust times as necessary. Layered Meal Instructions: Pre-heat OVEN to 350°F and layer starch on the bottom of the pot with recommended amount of water per the package cooking instructions. Insert the rack and lay protein and vegetables on rack. Close lid and bake according to chart below.

Quick Cooking (9 Minutes or Less)

Protein	Vegetable	Starch
Fish Fillets	Thin Asparagus and Thin Zucchini	Couscous
Small Chicken Cutlets	Bell Peppers	90-Second Microwave Rice
Frozen Shrimp/Frozen Fish Fillets	Haricots Vert	Israeli Couscous
	Spinach	Kasha
	Onions and Mushrooms	5-Minute Long Grain
	Pea Pods or Sugar Snap Peas	Wild Rice
	Frozen Peas	

Medium Cooking (10–20 Minutes)

Protein	Vegetable	Starch
Frozen Large Chicken Cutlets	Broccoli	10-Minute Quick Barley
Frozen Shrimp/Frozen Fish Fillets	Cauliflower	Farro
	Green Beans	Bulger
	Thick Asparagus	Quinoa
	Thick-Sliced Zucchini or Eggplant	10-Minute Rice

Longer Cooking (20+ Minutes)

Protein	Vegetable	Starch
Frozen Boneless Chicken Breast	Carrots	White Rice
Beef Roast (1½ inch or smaller	Sweet Potatoes	Jasmine Rice
if using steaming tray)	Parsnips or Turnips	Pilaf
Bone-In Meats, Chicken Thighs	Rutabagas	
	Artichokes	
	Corn on the Cob	

Pasta Cooking Chart–No Need to Drain!

For quick and easy pasta preparation that is ready in a snap without the time needed to boil and drain, look no further than your Ninja 3-in-1 Cooking System.

Simply follow the chart below, referring to the recommended cooking time on the box of the pasta. Find the cook time and amount of water needed to cook perfectly done pasta with no draining necessary.

Follow these directions:

Add the pasta, designated amount of water, 1-2 tablespoons butter, and 1 teaspoon of salt to the pot and gently stir to submerge pasta. Set OVEN to 250°F and set timer according to the chart below. Cook covered for 10 minutes, open, stir, cover, and cook for remaining time.

Pasta Cooking Chart			
1 Pound Box Recommended Cook Time	Water	Ninja Cook Time	Percentage of Time Saved with the Ninja*
4 minutes	2¾ cups	10–12 minutes	50% time savings
7 minutes	3 cups	15–18 minutes	33% time savings
9 minutes	3¼ cups	20–22 minutes	31% time savings
11 minutes	3½ cups	20–22 minutes	29% time savings

* Time to boil water (approximately 20 minutes) plus pasta cooking time.

Healthy Substitutions

Use this guide to see how you can make simple ingredient substitutions that will give your recipes a healthy boost.

	Healthy Swaps	
	Instead Of	**Substitute This**
DAIRY	Sour cream	Plain low-fat yogurt
	Milk, evaporated	Evaporated skim milk
	Whole milk	Fat-free milk
	Cheddar cheese	Low-fat cheddar cheese
	Ice cream	Frozen yogurt or sorbet
	Cream cheese	Neufchatel or light cream cheese
	Whipped cream	Light whipped topping
	Ricotta cheese	Low-fat ricotta cheese
	Cream	Fat-free half-and-half, evaporated skim milk
	Yogurt, fruit-flavored	Plain yogurt with fresh fruit slices
	Sour cream, full-fat	Fat-free or low-fat sour cream, plain fat-free or low-fat yogurt
PROTEIN	Bacon	Canadian bacon, turkey bacon, smoked turkey, or lean prosciutto (Italian ham)
	Ground beef	Extra-lean or lean ground beef, skinless chicken or turkey breast, tofu, tempeh
	Meat as the main ingredient	Three times as many vegetables as the meat on pizzas or in casseroles, soups, and stews
	Eggs	Two egg whites or ¼ cup egg substitute for each whole egg
OTHER	Soups, creamed	Fat-free milk-based soups, mashed potato flakes, or puréed carrots, potatoes, or tofu for thickening agents
	Soups, sauces, dressings, crackers, or canned meat, fish, or vegetables	Low-sodium or reduced-sodium versions

Healthy Substitutions

Use this guide to see how you can make simple ingredient substitutions that will give your recipes a healthy boost.

Healthy Swaps

	Instead Of	Substitute This
GRAINS	Bread, white	Whole-grain bread
	Bread Crumbs, dry	Rolled oats or crushed bran cereal
	Pasta, enriched (white)	Whole wheat pasta
	Rice, white	Brown rice, wild rice, bulgur, or pearl barley
FAT	Butter, margarine, shortening, or oil in baked goods	Applesauce or prune purée for half of the called-for butter, shortening, or oil; butter spreads or shortenings specially formulated for baking that don't have trans fats (Note: To avoid dense, soggy or flat baked goods, don't substitute oil for butter or shortening. Also don't substitute diet, whipped, or tub-style margarine for regular margarine.)
	Butter, margarine, shortening, or oil to prevent sticking	Cooking spray or nonstick pans
	Mayonnaise	Reduced-calorie mayonnaise-type salad dressing or reduced-calorie, reduced-fat mayonnaise
	Oil-based marinades	Wine, balsamic vinegar, fruit juice, or fat-free broth
SUGAR	Sugar	In most baked goods you can reduce the amount of sugar by one-half; intensify sweetness by adding vanilla, nutmeg, or cinnamon
	Syrup	Puréed fruit, such as applesauce, or low-calorie, sugar-free syrup
	Chocolate chips	Craisins
SAUCES	Soy Sauce	Sweet-and-sour sauce, hot mustard sauce or low-sodium soy sauce
SALT	Salt	Herbs, spices, citrus juices (lemon, lime, orange), rice vinegar, salt-free seasoning mixes or herb blends, low-sodium soy sauce (cuts the sodium in half (verify claim) by equal volume while boosting flavor)
	Seasoning salt, such as garlic salt, celery salt, or onion salt	Herb-only seasonings, such as garlic powder, celery seed, or onion flakes, or use finely chopped herbs or garlic, celery, or onions

Retail Accessory List

Baking Accessories

	Description	Brand Name	Size	Usage	Qty Fit in Ninja
	White porcelain. Oven to table serving. Good for souffles, personal-size quiches, desserts, and individual servings of sides.	BIA Blanc De Table	5" round	Quiches, souffles, sides, dips	2
	White porcelain. Oven to table serving. Good for souffles, personal size quiches, desserts, and individual servings of sides.	BIA Blanc De Table	6" oval	Crème brûlée	2
	Ramekins – White porcelain. Oven to table.	HIC	6 ounce each – 3½" round	Souffles	4
	Individual mini cupcake pans – metal	Foxrun	3¼" round	Cupcakes	4
	Individual mini cupcake pans – metal	Foxrun	2¼" round	Mini cupcakes	8
	Cake pops – fast and easy way to make cake pops. Includes food-grade nonstick silicone 2-piece tray, 50 sticks, and decorating guide. Use with any cake mix.	As seen on TV – TastyTop	8" x 5"	Cake pops	1 tray makes 8 pops
	Create a giant cupcake that the whole party can enjoy! Comes with 2-piece silicone cake pan and filling insert. Filling ideas – Ice cream, pudding, gelatin, fruit, candy, or whip cream.	As seen on TV – Big Top Cupcake	7½" round x 4"	Giant cupcake	1
	Petite stoneware dish for personal-size desserts and quiches. Multicolor.	Le Creuset	4¼"	Tarts, flans, quiches, meals	2
	Nonstick petite tart pan	Wilton	4" x ¾" round	Tarts, quiches	2
	6 oz. custard glaa cups	Anchor	3¾" x 2" round	Custards, mini cakes, reheating food	3

Retail Accessory List

	Description	Brand Name	Size	Usage	Qty Fit in Ninja
	Baking Accessories				
	Mini pie baking kit	Nordicware	7" round	Pies, pot pies, quiches, tarts	1
	6" round cake pan - Nonstick	WS - Goldtouch Nonstick	6" round	Cakes	1
	4" round cake pan - Nonstick	WS - Goldtouch Nonstick	4" round	Individual-size cakes	2
	2" timbale molds	William Sonoma	2" pans	Petite souffles, brioches, french cakes or popovers	6
	Silicone baking cups	Regency Silicups	4" round	Cup cakes, candy, muffins, quiches	6
	Silicone mini baking cups	Regency Silicups	2" round	Mini cupcakes, candy, muffins, quiches	12
	Disposable foil mini loaf pan	Durable Foil	$5\frac{5}{8}$" x $3\frac{3}{16}$" x $1\frac{15}{16}$"	Mini breads, cakes	2
	Disposable foil loaf pan	Durable Foil	8" x $3\frac{3}{4}$" x $2\frac{3}{8}$"	Breads, cakes, meatloaf	1
	Heart-shaped mini cake pan	Chloe Kitchen	3" x $3\frac{1}{4}$"	Mini cakes	4
	4" tube pans	Chloe Kitchen	4" round	Mini cakes	2
	Mini loaf pan. Nonstick.	Chloe Kitchen	$5\frac{1}{2}$" x $2\frac{3}{4}$"	Mini breads and meatloaf	2

Retail Accessories List

Roasting Accessories

	Description	Brand Name	Size	Usage	Qty Fit in Ninja
	Oval au gratin dish – Porcelain. Oven to table.	Apilco	10" x 5½" x 11/3" high	Casseroles	1
	Disposable foil rectangle pan	Mainstays	6" x 8" x 2½"	Casseroles, roasts, chicken, fish	1
	Disposable foil rectangle pan	Mainstays	7.37" x 5¼" x 1¾"	Casseroles, roasts, chicken, fish	1
	Disposable foil pan	Hefty	8" x 4"	Meatloaf	1
	1.5 qt. round side dish	CorningWare	7½" x 2½" round	Casseroles, roasts, chicken, fish	1
	Oval mini casserole dishes. Ceramic. Oven to table	CorningWare	5½" H x 3" x 2½"	Mini casseroles, sides, onion soup	2
	Pouch pods. Silicone form. Floats in water during cooking.	Fusion Brands	3½" x 2½"	Poached eggs, frittata, baked goods	5
	Flexible grilling skewers	FireWire	24"	Meat, seafood, vegetable skewers	1
	Spice bags	Regency	4" x 3"	Flavor meats, chicken, fish, and vegetables	1

Retail Accessories List

Roasting Accessories

	Description	Brand Name	Size	Usage	Qty Fit in Ninja
	Flavor injector	BBB Exclusive	N/A	Meat and poultry	1
	Porcelain baking dishes	Home Eessentials & Beyond	5" x 5" square	Mini casseroles, hot dips, reheat	1
	Meat thermometer	Polder	N/A	Meat and poultry	1

Equivalents Charts

Weight Measurements

USA/UK	Metric
1 oz.	30 g
2 oz.	60 g
3 oz.	90 g
4 oz. (1¼ lb.)	125 g
5 oz. (⅓ lb.)	155 g
6 oz.	185 g
7 oz.	220 g
8 oz. (½ lb.)	125 g
10 oz	315 g
12 oz. (¾ lb.)	375 g
14 oz.	440 g
16 oz.	500 g
1½ lb.	750 g
2 lb.	1 kg.
3 lb.	1½ kg

Length Measurements

⅛ in.	3 mm
¼ in.	6 mm
½ in.	12 mm
1 in.	2.5 cm

Liquid Measurements

USA	METRIC	UK
2 tbsp.	30 m	1 fl. oz.
¼ cup	60 ml	2 fl. oz.
⅓ cup	80 ml	3 fl. oz.
½ cup	125 ml	4 fl. oz.
⅔ cup	160 ml	5 fl. oz.
¾ cup	180 ml	6 fl. oz.
1 cup	250 ml	8 fl. oz.
1½ cups	375 ml	12 fl. oz.
2 cups	500 ml	16 fl. oz.

Abbreviations

USA/UK	Metric
oz = ounce	g = gram
lb = pound	kg = kilogram
in = inch	mm = millimeter
ft = foot	cm = centimeter
tbsp = tablespoon	ml = milliliter
tsp = teaspoon	l = liter
fl oz = fluid ounce	
qt = quart	

Recipes by Cooking Function

 STEAM INFUSED ROASTING

 FAST ONE POT MEAL MAKING

Recipes by Cooking Function

 SEARIOUS SLOW COOKING

 STEAM INFUSED BAKING

Recipes by Cooking Function

STOVETOP OR
OVEN COOKING

Index

Index

Index

Index

NINJA®

RULE THE KITCHEN®